Gourmet Glasgow

simple recipes for an easy life

First published 2003
by Black & White Publishing Ltd,
99 Giles Street, Edinburgh EH6 6BZ

ISBN 1 902927 83 4

British Library Cataloguing in publication data: a catalogue record for
this book is available from The British Library.

Printed and bound in Spain by Bookprint, S.L., Barcelona

The Editor thanks . . .
Alan Donaldson
Glasgow City Council
Greater Glasgow & Clyde Valley Tourist Board
Bill Neish MBE
Scottish Enterprise Glasgow
All chefs, patrons, contributors, colleagues and friends of the GRA
All at Black & White Publishing

Contents

all recipes serve 4

Introduction

If you're reading this as a Glaswegian, you will already be anticipating the treat ahead of you; if you are a visitor to the city, you have a culinary feast in store! Glasgow is now the envy of many European cities for its amazing and eclectic restaurant and café scene. Add to that its great shopping, outstanding Victorian architecture and plethora of cultural attractions, and it's easy to see why Glasgow is such a tantalising experience. No wonder one critic suggested that 'Glasgow is the Barcelona of northern Europe'.

Fifty years ago Glasgow was a grey and industrial city, and it would have been extremely difficult to imagine its current status as a trendsetter in European culture and a centre of dining excellence. It was not until the late 70s and early 80s that things really began to take off, but the emergence of the 'new' Glasgow dining scene can be traced back to such glamorous establishments as The Grosvenor in Gordon Street, The Whitehall in Renfield Street and The 1-0-1 and Malmaison in Hope Street. Luigi, the infamous maître d' at 'The Mal', resplendent in morning coat at lunchtime and full tails for dinner, typified the opulence of dining in the 40s and 50s. Famous Glasgow stalwarts including The Buttery and Rogano still held sway, but generally the choice (for what were only affluent customers in those days) was still very limited. Change, however, is always around the corner and along came a certain Mr Reo Stakis who, in a short space of time, transformed the entire ethos of eating out, not only in Glasgow but also across the length and breadth of Britain. The Stakis Steakhouses of the late 60s opened the doors of eating out to a hungry and expectant mass market.

Progress continued in the mid-70s with the arrival of more individually entrepreneurial establishments like The Fountain, La Bonne Auberge, Poachers, The Pendulum and The Ubiquitous Chip in the West End, and The Colonial and The Duke of Tourraine in the east. There was no stopping the tide of change and before long trendy restaurants and style bars appeared, amongst them Charlie Parkers and The Provençal, Smiths, Gatsby's and Lautrec's Wine Bar and Brasserie in Woodlands Terrace. The many excellent and diverse international establishments, including La Parmigiana, Ashoka and Amber Regent, would provide the platform and inspiration for modern-day Glasgow's remarkable dining culture.

The forementioned establishments by no means represent a comprehensive list, and readers will undoubtedly have personal favourites and fond memories of other pioneering Glasgow restaurants.

Located within an hour's drive of fresh oysters from Loch Fyne and the grazing glens of Perthshire, Glasgow has the world's best produce at its fingertips. The rest of the world clamours to buy, at a premium, Scotch beef, smoked salmon and fresh Atlantic seafood – we have it on tap.

Today Glasgow has the metropolitan feel of a major international city but still retains a sense of 'village' community. The restaurateurs in our city all understand that local spirit is a vital factor in presenting a town that is 'together'. Sharing experiences and knowledge is a culture in Glasgow, allowing us to progress at a pace which many spectators observe with envy.

The Glasgow Restaurateurs Association has grown over several years from a small number of restaurants to nearly 50 members to date. Of these members, all must fulfil certain exacting criteria and specific standards to be eligible. The Association has uniquely allowed a group of widely diverse professionals to exchange ideas with a common aim – to promote the excellence that is the Glasgow restaurant scene. With this in mind, how better to share our successful partnership than with the discerning diners and aspiring chefs in their own kitchens?

High standards are expected. High standards are achieved. The famous New York restaurateur, Danny Meyer, President of the Union Square Hospitality Group, said on a recent visit: 'I am enormously impressed with the exceptional quality of restaurants in Glasgow. The commitment to top-flight local ingredients, warm hospitality and compelling design make me want to return to Glasgow soon!'

Gourmet Glasgow is a whirlwind visit to many of Glasgow's great restaurants and a taste of the dishes you can find there. All the recipes have been selected with simplicity as a main ingredient and, of course, if you're not in the frame of mind for home cooking, you can easily visit the restaurant in question and sample the real thing!

Alan Tomkins

Visit www.bestglasgowrestaurants.com for additional information on all contributing restaurants

Breakfast

DESCRIBED IN THE DICTIONARY AS THE FIRST MEAL TO BE TAKEN IN THE DAY – QUITE LITERALLY TO BREAK THE FAST ASSOCIATED WITH SLEEP. HOWEVER THE FIRST MEAL OF THE DAY MEANS MANY THINGS TO MANY PEOPLE AND INDEED MAY BE TAKEN AT VARIOUS TIMES. OUR CHEFS HAVE PREPARED THEIR OWN PERSONAL SLANT ON THIS OVERLOOKED AND UNDERRATED MEAL – NO CEREAL AND TOAST LURKING HERE!

Café Gandolfi is a Glasgow institution. It is almost as famous for its stained-glass windows and Tim Stead furniture as it is for its delicious food, prepared with the best Scottish produce and infused with European flavour. Owner Seumas MacInnes is proud of 'Scotland's fantastic raw materials, from seafood to turnip'! Bar Gandolfi, upstairs, is perfect for rounding off the evening with an after-dinner refreshment.

café gandolfi

Cinnamon French Toast

with fresh fruit, Greek yoghurt and maple syrup

3 large free-range eggs
5 tbsp full-fat milk
½ tsp cinnamon
pinch of salt
enough fresh fruit, such as bananas,
  strawberries, raspberries and papaya, to give
  4 generous servings

90g unsalted butter
6 or more slices of brioche
300ml Greek yoghurt
6 tbsp maple syrup

Beat the eggs, milk, cinnamon and salt together until well blended. Allow the mixture to stand while you prepare the fruit.
Put a heavy-based frying pan on a moderate heat and melt the butter until it begins to splutter. Dip each slice of brioche
into the egg mixture and fry on both sides until golden brown.
Serve the French toast topped with a healthy dollop of Greek yoghurt and your chosen fruit drizzled with maple syrup.

frango

Chef John Gillespie is part of a team running one of Glasgow's top restaurants. His influences: 'Oriental food is simple and easily adapted to modern cooking techniques.' Frango's chic bistro style is perfectly suited to the cosmopolitan Italian Centre, in Glasgow's fashionable Merchant City.

Philosophy: consistently high-quality food and service.

Grilled Finnan Haddock
with black pudding, toasted crumpet and cheddar cream

a dash of white wine
4 fillets of smoked haddock, preferably Finnan
 haddock, with the middle and side bones cut
 out and fillets halved
4 slices of black pudding

300ml double cream
100g good-quality white cheddar, grated
4 crumpets
a handful of fresh flat leaf parsley

Put the white wine in a small pan and reduce by half.

Meanwhile grill the haddock and black pudding under medium heat.

Add the double cream to reduced wine, slowly bring to boil and whisk in the grated cheddar.

Toast the crumpets, put a slice of black pudding and 1 smoked haddock fillet on top of each of them, drizzle over the cheddar cream sauce and garnish with the flat leaf parsley.

Herb Omelette and Smoked Salmon
with cepes and a lime and chilli crème fraîche

200g cepes, sliced
vegetable oil, for searing
salt and pepper
5ml truffle oil
5ml balsamic vinegar
juice of ¼ of a lime
½ red chilli, de-seeded and diced
5g maple syrup
80g crème fraîche

14g fresh tarragon, chopped
14g fresh chives, finely diced
8 eggs, beaten
a little vegetable oil
200g smoked salmon
14g fresh chervil sprigs

Quickly sear the cepes in hot oil and then season them with salt and pepper. Mix the seasoned cepes with the truffle oil and balsamic vinegar and leave them to rest.

Mix the lime juice, finely chopped chilli, maple syrup and crème fraîche together.

Mix the tarragon and chives with the beaten eggs.

In a small pan, about 10cm in diameter, heat a little vegetable oil over a moderate heat. When the oil is hot, add a quarter of the beaten egg mixture and cook until it is just about set. Remove the small omelette from the pan and keep it warm while you repeat the process three more times.

Put a herb omelette on each of the 4 serving plates and top each of them with 50g of smoked salmon. Put a quarter of the mushrooms on top of the salmon.

Finish the dish with a serving of the lime and chilli crème fraîche and garnish with the sprigs of chervil.

the mariner

Coming from a line of good cooks, Gordon Dochard was 'well taught and heavily influenced' by his mother and great aunt, both skilled in the kitchen. The Mariner is renowned for its Scottish cuisine and flambé dishes, cooked at your table. Gordon loves the Glaswegians' 'banter and friendliness' – working in a restaurant in the heart of the city, he's in a prime position to enjoy its buzz.

Spicy Scrambled Eggs
with naan bread and sour cream

5g unsalted butter
1 tbsp red onion, finely chopped
1 tbsp button mushrooms, finely chopped
1 clove of garlic, peeled and chopped
$1/4$ tsp turmeric powder
$1/4$ tsp cumin powder
$1/4$ tsp ground coriander

12 eggs, beaten
salt and pepper
2 tbsp fresh coriander, chopped
1 tbsp plum tomatoes, finely chopped
4 small naan breads
4 tbsp sour cream

Heat a pan over a medium heat, add the butter and leave it to melt. Add the onion, mushrooms and garlic and cook for 2–3 minutes without allowing them to colour. Add the turmeric, cumin and ground coriander and cook for a further 2 minutes.

Pour in the beaten eggs and season to taste. Keep stirring until the eggs have softly scrambled. Add the chopped coriander and plum tomatoes, taste and, if necessary, adjust the seasoning.

Lightly warm the naan breads, carefully spoon the scrambled eggs over them and serve with the sour cream.

Influenced by Santa Fe and Mexico, Pancho Villas is one of the Merchant City's most popular restaurants. Vibrant colours, full-flavoured food and Latin music create a lively ambience. An extensive cocktail list specialising in margaritas and Mexican food with a modern spin ensure a great evening.

pancho villas

Huevos Rancheros

15ml olive oil
4 beefsteak tomatoes
2 medium onions, finely chopped
1 red chilli, finely chopped
1 small green chilli, finely chopped
1 green pepper, finely chopped

salt and pepper
1 bunch of fresh coriander, chopped
8 x 15cm ready-made corn tortillas
enough vegetable oil for frying
8 eggs

Blanch the tomatoes in boiling water, drain, peel, de-seed them and then cut them into small cubes.

Fry the finely chopped onion, chillies and pepper in the oil for 3 minutes until the onions have softened. Add the cubes of tomato and continue to fry for 5 minutes, then season with the salt, pepper and fresh coriander.

Shallow-fry the corn tortillas over a high heat until crisp. Remove the tortillas from the pan and keep them warm. Now, in a clean pan with a little vegetable oil, fry the eggs.

Put 2 tortillas on each serving plate, add 2 fried eggs to each plate and top with the salsa.

Poached Duck Eggs on Brioches
with asparagus and prosciutto salt

4 slices of prosciutto	4 duck eggs
4 brioche rolls	12 asparagus spears

Preheat the oven to 220°C.

Lay the prosciutto on a baking tray, put it in the oven and cook for 5 minutes until crisp.

Slice the tops off the brioches and then warm in oven for 1–2 minutes.

Poach the eggs in water for 4 minutes.

Poach the asparagus in salted water for 10 minutes and then refresh it in iced water.

Put the brioches on the 4 serving plates and top them with the poached duck eggs. Place 3 spears of asparagus and 1 brioche top alongside each of the brioches. Crumble the crispy prosciutto, scatter it over the plates and then serve.

Saint Jude's modern, comfortable elegance is reflected in its cooking – classic with a contemporary edge. Head chef David 'Looby' Sherry is glad to see 'global influences slowly being absorbed into the Glasgow food scene'. Fresh Scottish produce is allowed to offer its own flavour, not overpowered by heavy spice or jus.

Philosophy: an equal balance of traditional and contemporary styles on menus.

saint jude's

stravaigin

The Scots word 'stravaigin', meaning 'wandering about', provides inspiration for the three exciting venues. Each offers the best of Scottish hospitality and food, traditional and contemporary. Head chef Alan Doig is passionate about cooking and says, 'From the smartest restaurant to the tastiest street food – good food always inspires.'

Crisp Parmesan Polenta
with asparagus, serrano ham and poached duck eggs

2 tbsp olive oil
1 Spanish onion, diced
350ml water
salt and pepper
100g fine polenta

20g Parmesan, freshly grated
1 bunch of chives, chopped
8 slices of serrano ham
20 asparagus tips, blanched
4 duck eggs, poached

Heat a drizzle of olive oil in small pot over a medium heat and sauté the diced onion for 4–5 minutes. Pour 350ml cold water on to the softened onions, bring to the boil and add a pinch salt.

Slowly whisk the polenta into the boiling water and cook it until it is thick enough to stand a spoon in it. Remove it from the heat, stir in the Parmesan and chopped chives and season with pepper and more salt if required.

Spoon the polenta on to a flat surface, pat it down to a depth of 2cm and leave it to cool and set. Cut the polenta into squares and fry them in the remaining olive oil at a high temperature for 2 minutes on each side until crisp.

Place the crisp polenta on warm serving plates, top with ham, blanched asparagus tips and poached duck eggs. Drizzle with olive oil.

lunch

LUNCH – A MEAL EATEN DURING THE MIDDLE OF THE DAY. ASK A CROSS-SECTION OF THE POPULATION WHAT LUNCH MEANS TO THEM AND THE RESPONSE WILL BE AS VARIED AS OUR REPRESENTATIVE RESTAURANTS. THE DAYS OF MEAT, TWO VEG AND STEAMED PUDDING AND CUSTARD MAY BE A MEMORY BUT LUNCH CAN BE AS VARIED AS A TOSSED SALAD TO A ROAST JOINT – IF INSPIRATION IS WHAT IS REQUIRED TO SPICE UP YOUR EXHAUSTED REPERTOIRE, READ ON.

Seared Halibut Steak
with an orange and coriander risotto and tamarind butter

100g salted butter, softened at room
 temperature
50g tamarind pulp
25g salted butter or 1 tbsp vegetable oil
3 shallots, finely chopped
1 clove of garlic, peeled and crushed
2 oranges, peeled and divided into segments
150g risotto rice

10g coriander seeds, crushed
500ml fish stock
4 x 225g halibut steaks
50g fresh coriander leaves, roughly torn

Make the tamarind butter by putting the warm softened butter and the tamarind pulp in a mixing bowl and combining them thoroughly. Set the bowl aside at room temperature until you are ready to serve.

Heat the butter or oil in a frying pan and sweat off the chopped shallots, garlic and orange segments. Continue frying until the shallots have softened. Add the rice and crushed coriander seeds and sweat them off until the seeds are crackling. Gradually add the fish stock a ladleful at a time, giving the rice time to absorb the stock before adding more. Keep doing this until the rice is cooked but still has a bit of firmness to it.

Sear the halibut steaks for 1 minute on each side using a char grill. If a char grill is not available, melt 50g of butter in a heavy-based hot frying pan and fry for 3–4 minutes on each side.

Divide the risotto between 4 serving plates. Place the halibut steaks on top, drizzle the tamarind butter over the fish and scatter the coriander over the plates.

The Seafood & Grill is Bouzy Rouge's latest venue. It has fast become a popular place to dine, with a fantastic selection of the finest chargrilled Buccleuch steaks and the freshest Scottish seafood. Relax in comfort amid the splendour of the magnificent original Moorish tiles, complimented by gorgeous, warm interiors. Staff are friendly, professional and welcoming. Pre- and post-dinner drinks can be enjoyed in Bar Bouzy, which combines the grown-up atmosphere of a wine bar with stylish, contemporary interior design and music mixed to suit the mood. The perfect venue for a night out!

bouzy rouge seafood & grill

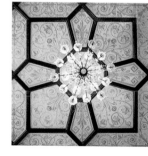

Café Andaluz brings a Spanish ambience and intimate sociability to Glasgow. Scottish and Spanish ingredients combine in eclectic modern and traditional delicacies. Philosophy: infuse tradition with sizzling Andalusian passion for a truly authentic experience.

café andaluz

Chorizo Frito Al Vino
(Spanish sausage, with red onion, in a red wine jus)

1 tsp olive oil
6 x 250g chorizo sausages, skinned and sliced
3 medium red onions, peeled and thinly sliced
salt
100ml red wine

150ml ready-made demi-glace (this is available in most supermarkets but you could use $\frac{1}{2}$ a beef stock cube dissolved in 150ml boiling water instead)
1 sprig of fresh thyme, roughly chopped

Heat the olive oil in a large pan to a moderate temperature, add the chorizo and fry until the sausage starts to brown.
Add the onions, with a pinch of salt, and fry until they soften.
Pour in the wine and allow it to boil briefly. Add the demi-glace or stock and stir. Keep stirring occasionally and allow the sauce to reduce.
Finally add the chopped thyme and serve.

Crab pasta
with chilli, lime and coriander

500g linguine (pasta in the form of small
ribbons)
1 tbsp olive oil
2 red chillies, chopped

juice of 1 lime
300g crabmeat
2 tbsp fresh coriander, chopped

Place the pasta in a large saucepan of salted boiling water, cook until al dente and drain.
Meanwhile, put the olive oil into a pan and warm it. Add the chopped chillies and lime juice and cook for a couple of
minutes. Next add the crabmeat and heat through before adding the coriander and finally the pasta.
Mix well and serve.

Salmon Napolitana

10 shallots, finely sliced
100ml olive oil
salt and pepper
100ml white wine
1 x 425g tin chopped tomatoes, drained
1 tbsp tomato purée
50g fresh basil, chopped

25g fresh parsley, chopped
25g fresh chives, chopped
800g salmon fillet, skinned
4 tomatoes, peeled, de-seeded and diced
100g button mushrooms, sliced
225g mozzarella, coarsely grated
200g crème fraîche

Cook the shallots in olive oil, season and add wine. Add the tomatoes and tomato purée and boil for around 15 minutes until the sauce thickens. Pass it through a conical strainer, add the herbs and leave it to cool.
Cut the salmon fillet into angled slices approximately 5mm thick. Arrange the salmon pieces on 4 lightly oiled ovenproof plates in a pizza shape with the thick edges outmost, using the salmon trimmings to fill any gaps at the centre of the dish.
Preheat the oven to 230°C.
Spoon the tomato sauce over the fish, spreading it out almost to the edge. Scatter the tomato dice, mushrooms and grated mozzarella on top of the sauce.
Bake the salmon for 5–6 minutes. Remove it from oven and spoon around the crème fraîche.

Roast Tuscan Sausages
with herb mash, mixed bean, tomato and tarragon stew

1 tbsp olive oil

1 medium onion, chopped

1 clove of garlic, chopped

100g smoked bacon, fat trimmed

2 tbsp tomato purée

800g tin chopped tomatoes

1 tsp sugar

8 Tuscan sausages (or you could use Toulouse sausages or chorizo)

100g mixed beans (such as chick peas, haricot beans, cannellini beans)

20g fresh tarragon, chopped

25g mixed fresh soft herbs (such as basil and tarragon), chopped

4 tbsp olive oil

500g potatoes (the Maris Piper variety works well), peeled, boiled and mashed

a handful of flat leaf parsley

Heat up a frying pan, add the oil and sweat off the onion, garlic and bacon. Add the tomato purée, tinned tomatoes and sugar, and gently simmer for 15–20 minutes.

Put the sausages in an ovenproof dish and roast them in a medium to hot oven (cooking time will vary depending on the size of the sausages you use).

Add the mixed beans and chopped tarragon to the onion and tomato stew and check for seasoning.

Liquidise the mixed soft herbs with the olive oil, add to the mash and check for seasoning.

Divide the tomato and bean stew equally between 4 serving plates. Put 2 sausages on each plate, top them with a quenelle of herb mash and garnish with the parsley.

Cacciucco

1 tbsp olive oil

1 large onion, finely diced

4 cloves of garlic, crushed

1 red or green chilli, sliced

50g fresh basil

2 fresh squid tubes, cleaned and cut into ½ cm
 pieces

500g monkfish, cut into 2.5cm pieces

4 king scallops

16 surf clams

20 prawn tails

8 fresh water king prawns

16 mussels

1 glass white wine

2 litres water

250g tomato purée

4 fish stock cubes

1 level tsp salt

1 tsp ground white pepper

4 portions of bread

In a large pot, heat the olive oil and then add the onion, garlic, chilli and basil. Once the onions are cooked, add the fish and the seafood, leaving the shells on, and cook over a medium heat for about 5–6 minutes. Next add the wine, water and tomato purée to the pan and, using a wooden spoon, keep stirring until the tomato purée has dissolved. Crumble in the stock cubes, add the seasoning and simmer for about 20 minutes.

Ladle the cacciucco into 4 large bowls and serve with the bread. Traditionally this is served with fettunta – toasted Italian bread that has been rubbed with garlic and virgin olive oil.

Mussel Stew
with asparagus, thyme and oysters

800ml fish stock
200ml white wine
400ml double cream
a pinch of salt
1 fresh bay leaf
2 bunches of asparagus, stems trimmed to
  about half their original length

1 tbsp vegetable oil, for frying
1 onion, peeled and finely sliced
2 sprigs of fresh thyme
300g mussel meat (you can buy this in jars)
8 oysters
salt and pepper

Make the fish cream by bringing the fish stock to the boil and reducing it to 200ml. Add the white wine and reduce again to 200ml. Now add the cream and the bay leaf and simmer gently until the sauce is of a pouring consistency. Cook the trimmed asparagus spears in boiling water for 2–3 minutes. Drain it, refresh it in cold water and absorb any excess water on some kitchen paper.

Heat the oil in a frying pan and sweat off the onion over a moderate temperature without allowing it to colour. Add the thyme and the fish cream, bring to the boil and then add the mussel meat. Cut the cooked asparagus tips in half and add them to the pan.

Open the oysters and divide them between 4 serving bowls and then pour the mussel stew over them. It is important not to boil the oysters as this will toughen them and make them rubbery.

Before serving, give the stew a quick flash under a hot grill.

Supreme of Corn-Fed Chicken
with banana bacon rolls and a tarragon butter sauce

500ml chicken stock
salt and pepper
4 corn-fed chicken supremes, with the skins
 still on

113g unsalted butter
3 bananas
6 rashers of smoked bacon
$1/2$ packet fresh tarragon, finely chopped

Preheat the oven to 180–200°C.

Put the chicken stock into a pan – one that is suitable for putting in the oven as well as going on top of the stove – and bring it to the boil. Season the chicken supremes and put them, skin side up, into the boiling stock, which should reach halfway up the supremes, and place a knob of butter on top of each one – you should use approximately half the butter for this. Dice the remainder of the butter and put it in the fridge to chill. Put the pan in the oven and cook the chicken for 20–25 minutes until the skins are golden.

Cut the bananas into 2.5cm pieces. Cut each rasher of bacon lengthways into two. Roll a bacon strip around each piece of banana and secure it with a cocktail stick.

When the chicken is ready, remove it from pan and put it aside to keep warm. Return the pan to the stove and reduce the cooking liquid by half.

Deep-fry the banana and bacon rolls for about 1 minute.

Add chopped tarragon to reduced stock.

Put a chicken supreme on each of the 4 serving plates along with 3 banana and bacon rolls.

Remove the stock from the heat, add the chilled diced butter and whisk until it is incorporated. Check the seasoning and coat the supremes with the sauce.

Steamed West Coast Mussels
with blue cheese and bacon

2kg mussels, cleaned
80g shallots, finely chopped
3 cloves of garlic, finely chopped
150ml dry white wine
80g blue cheese, cubed

150ml double cream
pinch of salt and pepper
120g unsmoked bacon, diced and cooked
1 tbsp fresh parsley, chopped
enough fresh crusty bread for 4

Put the mussels, shallots, garlic and white wine into pan, cover and place over a high heat for 3 minutes, shaking the pan occasionally.
Once the mussels start to open, add the blue cheese and the cream. Cover again and continue cooking for a further 2 minutes until the cheese melts and the cream bubbles. Discard any mussels that are still closed. Add the salt, pepper and bacon and give everything a good stir.
Ladle the mussels into warm bowls, garnish with parsley and serve with fresh crusty bread.

Yaki Udon

1 clove of garlic
15g fresh ginger, peeled
25ml soy sauce
20g granulated sugar
2 tbsp vegetable oil
250g chicken breast, cut into bite-sized cubes
1 carrot, peeled and cut into thin strips
1 courgette, cut into strips

$\frac{1}{2}$ red onion, peeled and cut into thin strips
$\frac{1}{2}$ bunch spring onions, sliced
$\frac{1}{4}$ red pepper, cut into strips
$\frac{1}{4}$ green pepper, cut into strips
$\frac{1}{4}$ yellow pepper, cut into strips
2 packs of udon noodles
10ml oyster sauce
red ginger, peeled and thinly sliced

To make the yaki sauce, crush the garlic and ginger together and then mix them into the soy sauce, along with the sugar.

Heat the oil in a wok until it is smoking and brown the chicken breast cubes. Add the strips of vegetables and cook for 2 minutes. Add the udon noodles and the oyster and yaki sauces and cook for a further 2 minutes.

Divide the dish between 4 serving plates and garnish with the red ginger.

oko

Colin Barr is one of a new crop of professional chefs taking Glasgow's restaurant scene to a new level. He 'enjoyed eating different food from a young age' and is influenced by Japanese and Greek cuisine. Oko's modern approach to Japanese food is refreshing and the mezzanine bar is ideal for chilling out in.

A relaxed, inviting atmosphere combines with innovative cuisine and the best Scottish produce for delicious modern dishes – poultry, seafood, venison and beef. Head chef David Clunas continues to improve the restaurant's high standards. 'I like to use fresh Scottish produce but I am influenced by the way people eat in the Mediterranean.'

papingo

Grilled Fillet of Salmon
with a creamy pancetta, pea and thyme sauce

4 good-sized salmon fillets
150g pancetta, in 1cm cubes
150ml white wine
250ml double cream

250g frozen peas
3 sprigs fresh thyme, finely chopped
salt and pepper

Preheat the oven to 220–225°C.

Put the salmon fillets on a buttered ovenproof dish, skin side up, and grill them until the skins start to colour and crisp up. Then put the ovenproof dish in oven for 7–10 minutes so that the salmon is cooked through. Remove the fish from the oven and set it aside to keep warm.

Cook the pancetta in a wide saucepan, without using any oil or butter, until it is crispy. Drain off any excess fat from the pan. Pour in the white wine and let it bubble away until it has reduced by around two-thirds. Add the cream, bring back to the boil and let it reduce again until it has a sauce consistency. Add the peas and thyme, cook for 2–3 minutes and season to taste.

Place a cooked salmon fillet on each of 4 warm serving plates, pour over the sauce and serve.

Pan-Seared
with basil aioli potatoes, baby

600g unpeeled new potato
  boiling water until tender
1 bunch of spring onion, sli
100g shallots, diced
100g fresh basil, shredded
150ml of mayonnaise
salt and pepper
4 cherry tomatoes on the vi

Dice the potatoes and put them i
everything together and set aside
Remove the stalks from the vine to
and keep them warm until you are
Put the veal jus in pan, warm it up
Put the baby spinach in a bowl, se
Season the fish on both sides. He
add the olive oil. Add the fish to th
cook for a further 2 minutes on the
Put some of the potato mixture on
bream fillet on top of the spinach a
some chervil to garnish – enjoy.

Seared Calves' Liver
with parsnip purée, crisp shallots and a herby orange dressing

4 medium parsnips, peeled and cores removed
50g unsalted butter
salt and pepper
100ml olive oil
2 cloves of garlic
zest of 1 orange

a handful of fresh basil leaves
a handful of fresh parsley leaves
4 slices of calves' liver
6 shallots, peeled and sliced into rings
a little seasoned flour

Simmer the parsnips in lightly salted water until soft. Drain the parsnips, put them in a blender or food processor with the butter, purée until smooth, season, remove and keep warm.

To make the dressing, blitz the olive oil, garlic, orange zest and herbs in a blender or food processor until combined. Heat a large frying pan until very hot and add a drizzle of oil. When the oil is smoking, reduce heat a little, season the calves' liver and sear for 1 minute on each side. (This will mean the liver will be rare so cook for slightly longer if you prefer.) Remove the liver from the pan and keep warm.

Toss the shallots in seasoned plain flour and deep fry until golden.

Spoon a mound of parsnip purée on to each of 4 warmed plates, top with a slice of liver and scatter some crispy shallots over the plate. Drizzle the dressing around the liver and over the top.

Salmon Coulibiac
with asparagus and lemon cream

15g fresh yeast
400ml full-cream milk
4 eggs, beaten
200g salted butter, softened
500g strong white flour
100ml dry white wine
juice of 1 lemon
500ml double cream
seasoning
500g long-grain rice, cooked

25g fresh dill, chopped
25g fresh chervil, chopped
4 eggs, hard-boiled
25g crème fraîche
1 egg, beaten
salt to taste
1 salmon fillet weighing about 1kg
1 bunch of asparagus, stems trimmed
100ml water

To make the pastry, mix together the yeast, milk, beaten eggs and butter in a bowl and then combine this with the flour. Cover the bowl and set it aside in a warm place.

Put the wine and lemon juice in a saucepan over a moderate heat and simmer until the volume has reduced by half. Add the cream and continue heating until the volume has reduced by half again and then season the sauce.

In a separate bowl, mix together the cooked rice, herbs, hard-boiled eggs and crème fraîche.

Roll the pastry out to give a thickness of $^3/_4$cm and put half of the rice mixture in centre of it, spreading it out so that it is the same shape as the salmon fillet. Place the salmon on top of the rice and then cover the fish with the remaining rice mixture. Pull the pastry up over the salmon so that it overlaps by 2cm. Trim away any excess pastry. Turn the salmon parcel over so that the seam is underneath, glaze the pastry with a mixture of 1 egg yolk and a splash of cream, place it on a baking tray and allow it to rest in the fridge for 1 hour.

Meanwhile, cook the asparagus in the boiling water until it is just tender. Drain it and then refresh it in iced water. Preheat the oven to 180°C and bake the salmon for 40 minutes.

Trim the ends off the coulibiac and slice it into 4 pieces. Put a few asparagus spears on each of 4 serving plates. Put a slice of coulibiac on top of the asparagus, pour over a little sauce and serve.

Khai Jiaw Hoy Naang Rom
(Thai omelette)

250g pork, minced
freshly ground black pepper
3 tbsp rice flour
$\frac{1}{2}$ tsp salt
125ml warm water
4 tbsp coconut oil
1 shallot, very finely sliced

1 clove of garlic, very finely sliced
2 tomatoes, very finely sliced
1 spring onion, very finely sliced
$\frac{1}{2}$ tsp coriander leaves, finely chopped
3 eggs, beaten
2–3 fresh big red chillies, shredded

Season the minced pork with the ground black pepper.

Put the rice flour in a mixing bowl, add the salt and the warm water and mix to produce a thin batter.

Heat the coconut oil in a heavy-based frying pan and pour in the batter. Cook the batter for about 2–3 minutes until it is three-quarters cooked.

Put the minced pork, the finely sliced shallot, garlic, tomato and spring onion, and the chopped coriander leaves into the pan and cook at a moderate temperature for 1–2 minutes.

Add the beaten eggs to the pan and continue cooking until the egg has set. Flip one edge of the omelette in towards the middle of the pan and then flip the other edge over on top to form an oblong shape.

Transfer the omelette to a serving plate and garnish with the shreds of fresh red chilli.

Monkfish, Oregano Cream and Roasted Peppers

4 fillets of monkfish, cut into 4cm cubes
175ml white wine
Maldon sea salt
black pepper
handful oregano, roughly chopped
200ml double cream

1 red pepper, cored and cut into irregular strips
1 green pepper, cored and cut into irregular strips
1 yellow pepper, cored and cut into irregular strips
a splash of olive oil

Preheat the oven to 180°C.

Put the monkfish cubes in an ovenproof dish with half of the white wine, season with salt and pepper and cover with tinfoil. Bake for 10 minutes.

Have a mouthful of the rest of the wine and put the remainder in a pan with the oregano and season. Allow the mixture to reduce over a high temperature for 5 minutes. Now add the cream and bring it to the boil. Take the pan off the heat and put it to one side.

Place the pepper strips on a baking tray, splash them with olive oil and add seasoning. Put them under a hot grill for 5–10 minutes, until the skins are dark brown, and then leave to one side.

Take the monkfish out of the oven and return the oregano and cream sauce to the hob on a low heat. Pour the wine from monkfish into the sauce and bring it back to the boil. Divide the fish between 4 plates. Pour the sauce over it and garnish with the grilled peppers, which are lovely served hot or cold.

dinner

DINNER – THE DICTIONARY CONTRADICTS ITSELF IN DESCRIBING DINNER AS A MEAL TAKEN IN THE EVENING BUT ALSO AT MIDDAY – SUFFICE TO SAY THAT IT IS VIEWED AS THE MAIN EVENT IN THE CULINARY DAY AND AS SUCH DESERVES SOME INNOVATIVE AND PERHAPS GUEST-IMPRESSING IDEAS. KEEP IT SIMPLE, THAT IS THE PHILOSOPHY – LESS IS MORE – IN THIS CASE LESS TIME IN THE KITCHEN, MORE TIME ENJOYING THE FRUITS OF YOUR LABOUR.

Crispy Prawn Balls

300g water chestnuts, minced
2 scallions, minced
1 thumb-sized piece of fresh ginger, minced
1kg prawns, cleaned, de-veined and chopped
  into tiny pieces
salt and pepper

whites of 5 eggs
$^1/_2$ tbsp yeast
3 tbsp plain flour
$^1/_2$ loaf bread, cut up into small cubes
600g vegetable oil

Mix the minced water chestnuts, scallions and ginger together and rub the mixture into the prawns. Put the salt, pepper, egg whites, yeast and flour in a bowl and mix it all together. Add the coated prawns and mix. Put the cubed bread in a bowl. Divide the prawn mixture into balls and roll them on the bread until each ball is covered in bread cubes.

Heat the vegetable oil in a wok. When it is hot, slowly deep-fry the prawn balls until golden brown and serve.

Pappardelle all Certosina
(flat ribbon pasta with king prawns and asparagus)

300g pappardelle pasta (use the Deco or Barillo
 brands if possible)
300ml water
20g salt
50ml olive oil
1 tsp garlic purée
20 king prawns, shelled and butterflied

12 asparagus tips, cooked and sliced
salt and coarse black pepper
25ml brandy
285ml double cream
1 pinch of saffron powder
30g fresh basil, chopped
50g fresh parsley, chopped

To cook the pasta, fill a large pot with the water (the golden rule for cooking pasta is that, for 1000g of pasta, you use 8–10 litres of water and 50g of salt), add the salt, bring to the boil and then add the pasta. Recommended cooking time for al dente pasta is 3–7 minutes from the time the water comes back to the boil.

Heat a large frying pan, add the olive oil, reduce to a low heat and add the garlic purée and fry until golden brown, making sure it does not burn. Add the king prawns and fry until they are firm in texture and slightly browned, stirring occasionally.

Now add the sliced asparagus tips and increase heat, adding a touch of salt and pepper. Throw in the brandy, allowing it to flambé, then pour in the cream, allow the liquid to thicken and reduce the volume slightly. Turn down the heat again, add the saffron and reduce to a creamy texture. Taste and add more salt and pepper if required.

Strain the pasta and add it to the sauce. Turn up the heat slightly, add the chopped basil and mix everything together. Once everything is bound together, use pasta tongs to divide it into 4 portions, ensuring the serving plates each have 5 king prawns on them, and finish off with a sprinkling of chopped parsley.

Aubergine Pakora

150g gram flour
½ tsp chilli powder
½ tsp salt
150ml natural yoghurt

1 tsp lemon juice
350g aubergine, sliced
enough vegetable oil for deep-frying
4 portions of tomato ketchup

Sift the gram flour into a bowl through a sieve, add the chilli powder and salt and mix it all together. Add the yoghurt and lemon juice and combine to form a batter.
Dip the aubergine slices into the batter and deep-fry them in hot oil until they turn golden brown.
Serve with the tomato ketchup.

ashoka west end

Chef Sanjay Majhu at the Ashoka West End is influenced
by traditional Indian cooking methods and produce: the
fruits of Kashmir, the seafood of Goa and hot dishes from
the scorching south.
The Ashoka philosophy: do it small, but do it good!

bouzy rouge

Chef Thomas Scott believes in combining his interest in visual art with rustic flavours for a sensual feast. Gaudi-influenced decor and an imaginative menu combine to give a stylish production, with a flexible mix-and-match approach.
Philosophy: casual, stylish gourmet dining!

Savoury Tomato Basil and Ricotta Cheesecake
with basil syrup

1 star anise
100g castor sugar
300ml water
100g fresh basil, finely chopped
150g oatcakes, crushed
25g unsalted butter, melted

300g ricotta cheese
40g sun-dried tomatoes
50g tomatoes, finely diced
a pinch of freshly ground nutmeg
a pinch of salt
a pinch of pepper

Put the star anise, castor sugar and water in a small saucepan, bring to the boil and then reduce to simmer with just small bubbles appearing. Remove from the heat, add half the basil and blitz with a hand blender.
Add melted butter to the crushed oatcakes and mix well. Put the mixture into a flan tin about 20cm in diameter (the oatcake base should be about half a centimetre thick). Then put it in the fridge to set for half an hour.
Put the ricotta cheese, sun-dried tomatoes, diced tomatoes, nutmeg, seasoning and the rest of the basil in a bowl and fold them together. Fill the flan tin with the mixture and push down firmly with a spoon. Turn the cheesecake out on to a plate and spoon the basil syrup round it.

Ceviche of Scallops and Tuna
with mangos, chilli and ginger

juice of 3 limes
juice of 3 lemons
2 mangos, finely chopped
200g tuna loin, cut into 1cm cubes
4 king scallops, cut into 1cm cubes
50g fresh coriander, chopped
1 red chilli, finely chopped

1 green chilli, finely chopped
25g fresh root ginger, peeled and grated
salt and pepper
150g rocket
1 lime, cut into wedges
1 lemon, cut into wedges

Put the lime juice, lemon juice, mangos, raw tuna, raw scallops, coriander, chillies, ginger and seasoning in a bowl and blend them together. Cover the bowl with cling film and allow it to stand for 2 hours in the fridge.
Divide the rocket between 4 serving plates, add the ceviche and garnish with the lime and lemon wedges.

Tortilla Española
(Spanish omelette with potato and onion)

6 eggs
a dash of olive oil
1 large onion, thinly sliced

salt
3 boiled potatoes, cut into slices about the
  thickness of a one-pound coin

Beat the eggs together in a large bowl. Heat the olive oil in a large, non-stick pan. Add the onions, with a pinch of salt, and sauté until translucent. Put the potatoes into the pan and lightly fry them. Now pour in the beaten egg and amalgamate it with the onions and potatoes. Beat lightly. As the ingredients heat, the eggs will start to thicken. When it has set, place the pan under the grill, or in a moderately hot oven (200°C), until it becomes golden brown. Place the omelette on a large plate.

Traditionally, it is cut into triangles and served with some fresh bread.

Vietnamese Rice Paper Rolls

50g mooli (white radish), cut into thin strips
50g carrot, cut into thin strips
50g onion, cut into thin strips
50g cabbage, cut into thin strips
2 tbsp vegetable oil
salt and pepper
50g sweet potato, peeled and grated
30g glass noodles
50g tofu (1 block), sliced
500ml vegetable oil for deep-frying
a pinch of granulated sugar

15g peanuts, crushed and roasted
5g sesame seeds, roasted
8 sheets rice paper
8 leaves butter leaf lettuce
30g fresh herbs – basil, coriander, mint –
  chopped
5g fresh ginger, grated
a pinch of granulated sugar
120ml soy sauce
20g mixed leaves

In a wok, stir-fry the strips of mooli, carrot, onion and cabbage in the oil, season and cool.

Deep-fry the sweet potato, glass noodles and tofu separately, until they are crispy, and then mix them all together.

Now combine the deep-fried and stir-fried ingredients and season with salt and pepper, sugar, peanuts and sesame seeds.

Soften the rice paper by dipping it in hot water for a few seconds. Drain it and lay it out on a flat surface. Top each sheet with a lettuce leaf, 2 tsp of the fried vegetable and tofu mixture and some of the mixed herbs. Roll up the mixture tightly in the rice paper, taking care not to rip it, to form a sausage shape. Slice each roll in half diagonally.

Mix the grated ginger and sugar into the soy sauce and divide this between 4 small shallow dishes or ramekins.

Serve 4 halves to a portion, along with a dish of the ginger, sugar and soy sauce mixture and a few mixed leaves.

Seared Pigeon Breast
with bean sprouts and balsamic dressing

4 tbsp balsamic vinegar
Maldon sea salt
cracked black pepper
10 tbsp olive oil
8 cherry tomatoes, cut into quarters
8 balsamic onions, cut into quarters (you can
  buy these ready-made)
25g fine yellow curly endive

1 small yellow pepper
8 plump pigeon breasts
2 medium carrots, peeled and cut into thin
  strips
100g bean sprouts
3 tbsp toasted sesame oil
20 sprigs fresh chervil

Reduce the balsamic vinegar by boiling it in a small saucepan until it has a syrupy consistency. Take the pan off the heat and add the salt, pepper and 7 tbsp of the olive oil and mix them in to the reduced balsamic vinegar. Leave the dressing to cool.

Arrange the tomato and balsamic onion quarters and the curly endive around the edge of the 4 serving plates. Cut the pepper into fine strips and soak them in iced water – this will cause them to curl – and put them aside until you are ready to serve.

Season the pigeon breasts. Pour the remaining 3 tbsp of olive oil into a hot pan. Cook the pigeon breasts for 2–3 minutes on each side or until they are pink in the centre. Remove the pigeon breasts from pan and allow them to rest. Using the same pan, gently stir-fry the carrot strips and the bean sprouts. Season and finish with the toasted sesame oil. Cut the pigeon breasts in half lengthways and slice them up. On the prepared plates, put alternate layers of the carrot and bean sprout mixture and pigeon breast slices in the centre of each. Drizzle the balsamic dressing over the tomatoes, balsamic onions and curly endive. Garnish the curly endive with sprigs of chervil and place the curled yellow pepper strips on top of each plated pigeon breast.

This is an intimate restaurant in a
landmark city-centre hotel, with
faultless food and discreet, friendly
service. Top-quality international
cuisine is prepared by James Murphy,
'inspired by ingredients to come up
with new recipes'.
Philosophy: a return to classic
standards.

camerons

gamba

Fresh seafood, such as monkfish, lobster and
halibut, is prepared to perfection by head chef Derek
Marshall, complemented by a slick front-of-house
team. 'Our goal is to maintain a busy, consistent
restaurant.' Striking contemporary Mediterranean
decor completes the experience.
Philosophy: outstanding cuisine, fresh and simple.

Scallop Salad
with lemongrass dressing and Parmesan shavings

450ml vegetable or sunflower oil
1 tbsp granulated sugar
2 tbsp white wine vinegar
1½ tsp English mustard
¼ onion, chopped
½ clove of garlic, crushed
1 tsp salt
150g rocket leaves
150g spinach
1 lollo rosso, picked
salt and pepper

250g ready-made apple jelly
2 cloves of garlic, crushed
1 red chilli, de-seeded and finely chopped
juice of 3 limes
2 balls stem ginger (this is available in syrup in jars), grated
1 bunch of lemongrass, outer layers removed and inner layers very finely chopped
1 tbsp vegetable oil
16 large scallops
100g Parmesan, for shaving

To make the 'Gamba' salad dressing, mix the vegetable or sunflower oil, sugar, white wine vinegar, English mustard, onion, garlic and salt together. Put the mixture into a blender, whizz and then pass it through a sieve. This quantity will be more than you need for this recipe so pour the remainder of the dressing into a screw-top bottle or jar and store it in the fridge.

Wash all the leaves, dry them in a salad spinner and put them into a large bowl. Add 2 tbsp of the 'Gamba' salad dressing and some salt and pepper. Mix everything together with your hands and divide the dressed leaves between 4 bowls.

On a low heat, warm the apple jelly in a pan with the garlic, chilli, lime juice and grated stem ginger balls. When the jelly has dissolved, remove the pan from the heat, add the finely chopped lemongrass and liquidise. Leave the dressing to cool before passing it through a sieve.

Put the oil in a hot frying pan and, when it starts smoking, add the scallops. Keeping the heat high, allow the scallops to cook for 1–2 minutes on each side.

Remove the scallops from the pan and arrange them on dressed leaves. Using a potato peeler, shave the Parmesan over the salad. Finally, lightly dribble the lemongrass dressing over the whole salad. This has quite a strong flavour so only a little will be required.

Aubergine Fritters

200g gram flour
³/₄ tbsp salt
¹/₂ tbsp chilli powder
¹/₄ tbsp turmeric
³/₄ tbsp cumin seeds
¹/₂ tbsp coriander seeds

2 medium aubergines, sliced
1 litre sunflower oil
4 portions of fresh salad
1 pot of fresh natural yoghurt

Sieve the gram flour into a large bowl. Add the salt, chilli powder and turmeric. Lightly crush the cumin and coriander seeds together using a mortar and pestle. Add the crushed seeds to the bowl and mix them into the spiced flour. Combine all the ingredients together with enough water to make a smooth batter.

Dip the aubergine slices into the batter and deep-fry them in the sunflower oil at a temperature of 160°C until golden brown.

Place some salad on each of the 4 serving plates. Place the aubergine fritters on top and put some natural yoghurt on the side.

Mother India's Abdul Hameed uses fresh herbs and plenty of originality to create Indian dishes with flair. He 'enjoys the lively atmosphere in the kitchen'. With a 21st-century approach to the traditional Indian buffet, each dish is prepared to individual requirements.

Philosophy: relaxed Indian dining.

mother india

mussel inn

The Mussel Inn, owned and run by shellfish farmers, takes pride in sourcing produce from the very best suppliers. Simple, appetising fish and seafood dishes are served up in the informal restaurant. Mattias Johansson's passion for cooking runs in the family. He finds Mediterranean seafood inspiring and his professional goal is to 'present shellfish in such a way that people are willing to trust us with their first taste of it and come back for more'.

Pan-Fried King Scallops
with sesame oil on a herb salad with cherry tomatoes

mixed leaves, such as rocket and spinach
  (mixed bags are available in most
  supermarkets)
30g fresh herbs (coriander and flat leaf parsley
  work well)
4 tbsp lemon juice

5 tbsp sesame oil
12 good-sized king scallops
16 whole cherry tomatoes
salt and pepper
chives to garnish

Toss the mixed leaves and herbs together with the lemon juice and 1 tbsp of the sesame oil. Place equal amounts of the dressed salad leaves in the centres of the 4 serving plates.

Heat a pan with the rest of the sesame oil until it is very hot. Put the scallops in the pan and fry them for 30 seconds on each side. Add the cherry tomatoes, fry for a further 30 seconds and season with salt and pepper.

Arrange the scallops on top of the mixed leaves and place the cherry tomatoes around the outside of the leaves. Drizzle the oil from pan round the plates and over the scallops. Garnish with whole chives.

Mixed Tempura
with a chilli dipping sauce

50ml wine vinegar
40ml soy sauce
10ml sesame oil
$1/2$ tbsp chilli powder
1 egg, beaten
100ml cold sparkling water
about 90g tempura flour
1 yellow pepper, cored and cut into large
  chunks

1 red pepper, cored and cut into large chunks
$1/2$ sweet potato, peeled and sliced
4 mushrooms
$1/4$ aubergine, sliced
8 king prawns, shelled but with the tails still on
½ litre vegetable oil

To make the chilli dipping sauce, mix the wine vinegar, soy sauce, sesame oil and chilli powder together and leave the ingredients to infuse in the fridge for at least 2 hours.
Add the egg to the cold water and slowly blend in enough flour to give a batter of a consistency that is thick enough to coat vegetable pieces.
Roll the vegetables and prawns in some flour and then dip them into the batter mix.
Heat the vegetable oil in a deep pan, deep-fat frier or chip pan until it is very hot and fry the battered vegetable pieces and the king prawns in batches.
Drain the tempura on some kitchen paper and serve with the dipping sauce.

Fillet of Sea Bass
on crab salsa

1 red onion, peeled and finely chopped
$1/2$ red chilli, finely diced
1 ripe mango, chopped into small pieces
4 vine tomatoes, peeled, de-seeded and
  chopped
10 fresh basil leaves, torn into small pieces
150ml virgin olive oil

juice of 2 limes
225g fresh white crabmeat
1 avocado, peeled, de-stoned and sliced
4 fillets of sea bass, scaled and pin-boned
rock salt

Mix the onion, chilli, mango, tomatoes, basil and half of the olive oil together in a bowl. Add the juice of 1 of the limes and leave the bowl to stand at room temperature for 1 hour. Then divide this mixture between 4 serving plates, placing it in the middle of the plates. Sprinkle the crabmeat over it and fan out the avocado slices on top of the crabmeat. Brush the sea bass fillets with the remainder of the olive oil and sprinkle them with rock salt. Grill the fish for 6 minutes on high without turning them.

Place a fillet of sea bass on top of each fan of avocado, drizzle the rest of the lime juice over them and serve.

With effortlessly stylish surroundings and impeccably smooth
service, Opus is inspired by classic dishes and spices from around
the world. 'Good food is a concoction of skill and produce.'
Philosophy: relaxed fine dining, with light food and mood.

opus

At La Parmigiana, unrivalled standards are achieved by head chef and owner Sandro Giovanazzi. He combines Mediterranean influences with an expert knowledge of the Scottish hunting season, demonstrated in his delicious seafood and game dishes.

Philosophy: serving the highest quality of food in an unpretentious manner, in comfortable surroundings.

la parmigiana

Fresh Egg Tagliatelle
with wild mushrooms

300g plain flour, plus some extra for dusting
1 tbsp extra-virgin olive oil
2 whole eggs and 3 yolks
6 tbsp extra-virgin olive oil
200g mixed wild mushrooms, roughly chopped

2 cloves of garlic, chopped
30g fresh flat leaf parsley, chopped
salt and pepper to taste
100g Parmesan cheese, freshly grated

Mix the plain flour, olive oil, eggs and yolks in a food processor and blitz them together. Remove the mixture from the food processor and knead it until you have a smooth elastic dough. Wrap the pasta dough in cling film and refrigerate for 1 hour.

Using a pasta machine, roll the dough into very thin sheets, dusting with flour as necessary. Now cut the sheets into ribbons or tagliatelle, with a cutting attachment, and put them aside.

Bring large pot of salted water to the boil.

Meanwhile, heat a large frying pan, add the olive oil and heat until it reaches a temperature that will sizzle the mushrooms. Add the mushrooms first and cook for 30 seconds and then add the garlic and 20g of the parsley (otherwise the garlic and parsley will burn). Season. If you see that the mushrooms are browning too much, add a few spoons of the water from the pasta pot.

When the water is boiling, add the pasta. Fresh pasta cooks very quickly. When it floats to the top, it is ready. Drain the tagliatelle, add it to the pan of mushrooms and mix well. Divide the mushrooms and pasta between the 4 serving plates and sprinkle each with the remainder of the chopped parsley. Serve with the grated Parmesan cheese.

Galette of Crab, Tomato and Courgette

200g fresh white crab meat
tbsp chopped chives
30g mayonnaise
6 plum tomatoes, blanched and peeled
2 courgettes, sliced to the thickness of one-
  pound coins

1 tsp thyme leaves
4 basil leaves, sliced finely or chopped
salt
fresh white pepper
extra-virgin olive oil
a few drops balsamic vinegar (optional)

Pick through the crab meat to check for bones, then mix in the chives and mayonnaise and season.

Toss the sliced courgettes in the thyme and olive oil and pan fry till golden brown. Allow to cool.

Slice 4 of the blanched tomatoes very thinly to get 10 slices from each.

Assemble 5 pieces of tomato and courgette in the bottoms of 4 small rings, such as pastry rings. The tomato and courgette should sit neatly in alternate overlapping slices in the bottom of each ring. Spoon a layer of crab meat on top, then repeat with another layer of tomato and courgette.

Evenly dice the rest of the tomatoes and mix with the basil leaves and some olive oil.

Carefully turn the individual galettes out onto 4 serving plates.

Drizzle the tomato, basil and olive oil mixture around the galettes and serve. Finish with a sprinkle of balsamic vinegar, if using.

étain

Discreetly located in the bustling city centre of
Glasgow, étain is a modern French restaurant.
Using the very best of Scottish produce, head
chef Geoffrey Smeddle has carefully created a
distinctive menu that exploits the finest, most
delicious seasonal ingredients available. Classic in
atmosphere with an intimate and elegant setting,
étain is pioneering in its fresh, international outlook.

Lemon and Thyme Roast Quail
with soft leek rosti and a port wine jus

4 sticks lemongrass, outer layers removed, inner layers chopped
4 cloves of garlic, crushed
50g fresh thyme, roughly chopped
100ml olive oil
4 whole quail, trimmed of excess skin
4 large potatoes, grated then washed
1 large leek, finely chopped
2 egg yolks

100g salted butter, softened
salt and pepper
1 tbsp vegetable oil for frying
500ml brown chicken stock or game jus
150ml port
30g redcurrant jelly
2 quail eggs, boiled, shelled and halved
4 sprigs of thyme

Mix together the lemongrass, garlic, thyme and olive oil, pour the mixture over the quail and refrigerate overnight.

In a bowl, mix the grated potato with the leek, egg yolks, butter and seasoning. Divide the mixture into 4 equal balls and then flatten them into disc shapes. Fry gently on both sides until light brown.

To make the sauce, heat the brown chicken stock or the game jus in a pan with the port and redcurrant jelly and let it cook until it has reduced to a consistency that will cover the back of a spoon.

Drain the flavoured oil from the quail and seal them off in a hot frying pan. There is no need to add oil to the frying pan as the quail will be oily enough.

Preheat the oven to 200°C.

Put the fried leek rosti in a roasting tin, place a quail on top of each one and roast for 15 minutes.

Put 1 quail and 1 rosti disc on the centre of each of 4 serving plates and pour some port wine jus round them. Garnish each plate with 2 boiled quail egg halves and a sprig of thyme.

78 st vincent

Chef Duncan McKay has been influenced by journeying through Europe and Asia. His travels have led him to work in Glasgow, which he describes as a lively and interesting city, with a culinary culture he is proud to be part of. 'Eating out should be viewed as an everyday activity, not reserved only for special occasions – reflected in the accessibility of 78's menus.'

amber regent

At the Amber Regent, owner Andy Chung takes pride in serving up 'authentic Chinese food because of its history, variety and creativity'. Fresh game is an inspiration. Plush decor and elegant surroundings complement traditional Cantonese and Szechuan cuisine.

Philosophy: to present Chinese food at its best, with the best of service, giving enjoyment to every customer.

Stir-Fried Scallops with Asparagus

1/2 tsp salt
1/2 tsp white pepper
1/2 tsp rice wine
1/2 tsp monosodium glutamate
1/2 tsp cornflour
227g scallops
1 litre water
1/2 tbsp malt vinegar
a little olive oil for stir-frying
1/2 tsp sesame oil

1/2 tsp white pepper
1/2 tsp monosodium glutamate
1/2 tsp granulated sugar
1/2 tsp salt
1/2 tsp cornflour
2 tsp water
227g asparagus, cut into 1–1 1/2-inch lengths
5 tbsp fresh ginger, finely sliced
1 tsp rice wine
5 carrots, sliced

Mix the salt, white pepper, rice wine, monosodium glutamate and cornflour together and marinate the scallops in this mixture for about 10 minutes. Put the water and vinegar in a pan and boil for 1 minute. Soak the marinated scallops in the hot water and vinegar for 1 minute, remove them from the water and absorb excess moisture on some kitchen paper.

Heat a little of the olive oil in a wok, add the scallops, stir-fry them for 3–4 minutes until they begin to colour, remove them and then set them aside.

Heat the sesame oil in the wok that the scallops were cooked in, add the white pepper, monosodium glutamate, sugar, salt, cornflour and water and cook for a minute or so until the sauce thickens.

Cook the asparagus in boiling water and boil for about 1 minute, drain it and then soak it in some clean cold water. Remove it from the water and absorb any excess water on some kitchen paper.

Heat some more olive oil in a clean wok, add the sliced ginger and stir-fry until it starts to turn golden, before adding the scallops and stir-frying again for 3 minutes. Add the rice wine, sliced carrot and cooked asparagus, stir-fry for a further 2 minutes and serve.

Pollo Peperonata con Pomodori Secchi

(chicken with peppers, onions and sun-dried tomatoes in a tomato sauce)

2 tbsp olive oil

4 skinned and boned chicken breasts, weighing
  about 175g each

150g plain flour

2 red onions, chopped

2 red peppers, sliced into rings

2 cloves of garlic, crushed

12 pieces of whole sun-dried tomatoes

1 x 175 ml glass of red wine

2 large tins of chopped peeled tomatoes

salt and pepper

Warm the frying pan with olive oil. Dust the chicken breasts with the flour to seal in the flavour and stop them sticking to the pan and fry them gently on the same side for 7–10 minutes. Turn, add the chopped onions, sliced peppers, garlic and sun-dried tomatoes and continue cooking for a further 5–10 minutes, stirring occasionally.

Now add half of the wine and both tins of chopped tomatoes. Keeping the pan on a medium heat, cook for a further 5–10 minutes or until the chicken is cooked and the sauce is a rich red colour, adding salt and pepper if required.

Serve with your favourite vegetables and some boiled potatoes.

Now you deserve the other half of that glass of wine.

At l'Ariosto, authentic Italian cuisine is prepared from specially imported ingredients and prime local fish and meat. Live entertainment, to accompany wining and dining, and surroundings that resemble a traditional village courtyard, provide an inviting atmosphere.

Chef and patron Giovanni Cecchehi's philosophy: 'Variety is the spice of life.'

l'ariosto

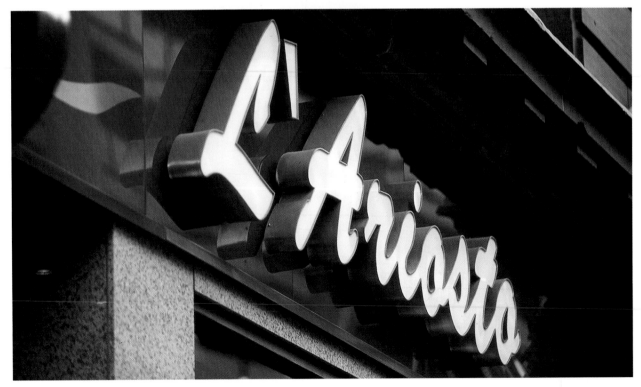

The culinary tradition of head chef Bhagwant 'Barry' Singh's native Punjab, and the secret spice blends his family has passed down the generations, have enriched the legendary curry experience to be enjoyed in this West End gem.

ashoka ashton lane

Chicken Jaipuri

3 large onions
275ml mustard oil
1 level tsp cumin
60g ginger purée
20g garlic purée
30g salt
1 tsp chilli powder
4 green chillies, chopped
1 tsp turmeric
2 tbsp tomato purée

1kg chicken fillets, chopped
2 tbsp ready-made tandoori paste (available in
    most Asian stores and some supermarkets)
550ml water
3 bell peppers of various colours, for
    presentation
2 tbsp vegetable oil
2 tbsp coconut cream
pinch of dried fenugreek
sprinkling of fresh coriander

Chop up 2 of the onions. Heat the mustard oil in a frying pan and lightly fry the onions until golden. Add the cumin, ginger purée and garlic purée and stir for 2 minutes before adding the salt, chilli powder, chopped green chillies, turmeric and tomato purée. Continue to stir until all the ingredients have been blended together.

Add the chopped chicken fillets and mix well. Continue to stir-fry until the chicken fillets are sealed and then blend in the tandoori paste. Add the water and simmer for about 5–10 minutes until the chicken is tender.

Meanwhile, chop the peppers and the remaining onion, lightly fry them in the vegetable oil until al dente. Remove the pan from the heat but keep warm.

Now slowly add the coconut cream to the chicken and stir for 1 minute. Add the fried peppers and onion and stir again. Garnish with a sprinkling of dried fenugreek and fresh coriander and serve.

Chicken Tikka Masala

120ml vegetable oil
1 large onion, finely diced and divided into 2
  equal lots
1$\frac{1}{2}$ tbsp cumin
1$\frac{1}{2}$ tbsp salt
4 tbsp fresh ginger, crushed
2 level tbsp fresh garlic, crushed
1$\frac{1}{2}$ tsp turmeric
1$\frac{1}{2}$ tsp curry powder
2 tsp chilli powder
pinch of dried fenugreek

2 tbsp tomato purée
800g chicken fillets
135ml water
1 large green pepper, diced
1 tsp ready-made tandoori paste (available from
  most Asian stores and some supermarkets)
250ml yoghurt
1 tbsp coconut cream
1 heaped tsp ready-made mint sauce
1 bunch of fresh coriander, roughly chopped

Heat the oil in a deep pan over a moderate heat and add one lot of diced onion together with the cumin and salt. Stir until the onions are golden brown and then add the ginger and garlic, blending well. Add all the remaining spices and the tomato purée, stir well and let this simmer on a low heat for 5 minutes.

Add the chicken pieces and mix well. Stir in the water, put a lid on the pan and simmer on a low heat for around 15 minutes, until the chicken is cooked through.

Add the remaining onions, together with the diced pepper, tandoori paste and yoghurt and replace the lid again. Let this simmer for another 5–10 minutes until the peppers are al dente. Now add the coconut cream and the mint sauce, stir well and allow to simmer for a further 30 seconds

To garnish, sprinkle the dish with the coriander. Your mouth-watering masala is now ready to serve.

Masala Chops

2 tsp ground cumin seeds
2 tsp ground coriander
$1/4$ tsp chilli powder
1 clove of garlic, crushed
salt
juice of 1 lemon

4 pork or lamb chops
4 portions of cooked pilau rice
4 portions of salad

Mix the cumin seeds, coriander, chilli powder, garlic and salt together. Make the masala paste by combining the mixture with the lemon juice.

Slash the chops on both sides, rub the masala paste into the meat and leave it to marinate in the fridge for 30 minutes.

Cook the chops under a moderate grill for 5–6 minutes on each side and serve with the rice and salad.

Fillet of Sea Bass
with crushed Jersey Royals, ratatouille and a herb oil

25g fresh chives, chopped
25g fresh basil, chopped
25g fresh flat leaf parsley, chopped
25g fresh coriander, chopped
250ml boiling water
250ml olive oil
salt and pepper
400g Jersey Royals
salt and pepper
28g unsalted butter
a little vegetable oil
1 shallot, finely diced

$^1/_4$ aubergine, finely diced
1 clove of garlic, crushed
$^1/_2$ courgette, finely diced
$^1/_2$ red pepper, finely diced
salt and pepper
2 tomatoes, peeled, de-seeded and diced
a little vegetable oil
a small knob of butter
4 x 160g fillets of sea bass, seasoned with salt
  and pepper
100g fresh basil, roughly torn

First make the herb oil by plunging all the chopped herbs into the boiling water for 10–15 seconds. Drain off the boiling water and cool the herbs in some iced water. Drain well and mix with the olive oil. Put the herb and oil mixture into a liquidiser and blitz for a few minutes. Pass the liquidised mixture through a muslin cloth, season and store in a screw-top bottle or jar.

Boil the potatoes, drain, season, add the butter and crush them lightly with a fork.

Heat the vegetable oil in a small pot and sweat off the shallot until soft. Add the aubergines and garlic and continue to cook until the aubergines are soft but not coloured. Now add the diced courgette, diced pepper and seasoning. When heated through, add the tomatoes and continue cooking until the pan is semi-dry. Remove from the heat and keep warm.

Heat some vegetable oil in a frying pan over a fairly high heat. When the oil is very hot, add a small knob of butter. Once the butter foams, add the sea bass, skin side down, and fry for 3–4 minutes. Turn the fillets over and continue frying for a further minute or so. Remove the fish from the pan and allow it to rest in a warm place for a minute before serving.

Add the basil to the potatoes.

Put some potatoes in a ring on each of the 4 warmed plates. Put a fillet of sea bass on top of the potatoes and then place a spoonful of ratatouille on the side. Finally, drizzle the plates with herb oil.

la bonne auberge

Glasgow's original brasserie, La Bonne Auberge, fuelled by the passion of its staff, uses the finest French techniques and produce. Executive chef Gerry Sharkey is proud of 'close links between the industry and education . . . kids' cooking skills are improving'.
Philosophy: more quality, less quantity.

The diverse flavours of the Orient create a highly individual style of cuisine and a fresh, exotic range of fish, meat and vegetarian dishes. Donald Flanagan, originally from Ireland, has made Glasgow his adopted home and enjoys the local sense of humour: 'I've yet to see the statue of Wellington without a traffic cone on its head!'

café mao

Hunan Tiger Prawns

20ml peanut oil

50g red onion, sliced

50g bell peppers, de-seeded and cut into large
 dice

50g button mushrooms, quartered

50g mange tout

5g garlic, crushed

32 (about 600g) tiger prawns

60ml ready-made spicy soy bean paste

30ml ready-made oyster sauce

20ml soy sauce

30g pak choy

10g sesame seeds, roasted

500g jasmine rice, steamed and divided
 between 4 small bowls

30g spring onion, sliced

2 small shallots, finely sliced and fried

Stir-fry the vegetables and garlic in the peanut oil in a hot wok for 1 minute. Add the tiger prawns and cook for a further minute. Add the spicy soy bean paste, oyster sauce and soy sauce and continue to cook until the prawns are ready. Finally, add the pak choy, stir it in and cook for another 20 seconds.

Put the bowls of steamed jasmine rice upside down on each plate and remove the bowls. Arrange the prawns and vegetables around the rice and sprinkle the sesame seeds over them.

Finally, garnish the rice with the spring onion and fried shallots.

Seared Scallops
served with Avruga caviar, prawn custard and a vodka, orange and tomato sauce

200g Norwegian prawns
4 egg yolks
a pinch of paprika
a pinch of salt
a pinch of black pepper
250ml milk
250ml cream

1 25ml measure vodka
100ml tomato juice
100ml orange juice
50g unsalted butter
4 king scallops
4 tsp Avruga caviar

Preheat the oven to 160°C.

Put the prawns in a food processor with the egg yolks, paprika, salt and pepper and blitz for 30 seconds. Add the milk and cream and blitz for a further 20 seconds. Divide the prawn custard between 4 espresso cups. Put the cups in an oven tray and fill the tray with water so that is comes three-quarters of the way up the cups. Put the tray in the oven and cook for 35–40 minutes until set.

Heat the vodka, tomato juice and orange juice in a saucepan and reduce the liquid by half.

Heat a frying pan on the stove to a moderate temperature and add the butter. When the butter starts smoking, place the scallops in the pan, season them and cook for 90 seconds on each side.

Pour some sauce over each of the 4 serving plates. Put a seared scallop on each plate and carefully position a tsp of Avruga caviar on top of each scallop. Turn the custards out of the espresso cups and place one on the side of each plate.

Pan-Fried Sea Trout Fillet
with crushed lemon thyme potatoes and vine tomatoes

600g new potatoes
1 small bunch of fresh lemon thyme
4 meaty sea trout fillets
Maldon sea salt
cracked black pepper
6 tbsp olive oil
50g unsalted butter
juice of 1 lemon

2 large shallots, finely sliced
100ml double cream
6 fresh basil leaves, cut into fine strips
200g baby spinach
2 vine tomatoes, chopped into small cubes

Boil the potatoes in salted water, adding some lemon thyme sprigs to the water for flavour. When cooked, drain the potatoes and keep them warm.

Season the trout fillets with the sea salt and black pepper. Heat 3 tbsp of the olive oil and fry the trout fillets, skin side down, at a moderate heat for 4 minutes. Turn the fillets over and cook for a further 2 minutes. Remove the fish from the pan and allow them to rest in a warm place.

Add 10g of the butter and a dash of lemon juice to the pan the fish was cooked in, add a third of the shallots with some of the thyme sprigs and cook until the shallots have softened. Add another dash of lemon juice and the double cream and simmer slowly for 1 minute, allowing the juices in the pan to mix with the cream. Take the pan off the heat, whisk in another 10g of butter and then add the basil. Pour the contents of the pan into a blender and liquidise until smooth.

Sauté the remaining shallots with some thyme in a pan with another 20g of butter. Add this mixture to the potatoes, season and lightly crush the potatoes with a fork.

Sauté the spinach in the remaining 10g of butter until limp and then season it.

Take a warm serving plate and put a pastry ring in the centre of it. Fill the pastry ring with crushed potatoes and then remove the ring. Repeat this for the 3 other plates. Put some spinach on top of the potatoes and top with a trout fillet. Arrange some of the chopped tomatoes on the plate around the fillet before drizzling the sauce over the fish and around the plate.

Rendezvous of West Coast Seafood
with saffron and tomato sauce

fish bones and skin from 2 or 3 small fish such
  as sole or trout
  (or, if fish bones and skin are not available,
  use 250ml fish stock made using a little fish
  bouillon)
1 bouquet garni
500ml water
a few strands of saffron
30g unsalted butter
2 small shallots, finely chopped
1 tbsp Noilly Prat or Dry Vermouth
80ml dry white wine
200ml double cream
salt and pepper

2 medium tomatoes
4 king scallops
4 medium langoustine
16 mussels, washed and de-bearded
2 sole fillets, skinned, cut into 4 strips and
  rolled up
4 small rainbow trout fillets, skinned and rolled
  up
(You may substitute any of the above fish or
  shellfish but you must prepare it to a size that
  allows your selection to steam evenly
  together.)
4 sprigs of basil or other herbs for decoration

If using fish bones and skin, simmer them with the bouquet garni in the water for around an hour until it has reduced to 250ml. Strain it through a fine sieve or muslin into a bowl. If using fish stock, heat it to boiling point in a saucepan and pour it into a bowl. Now add the saffron strands to the bowl and leave it to infuse for at least 10 minutes.

In another saucepan, melt the butter, lightly sauté the shallots, add the Noilly Prat or Dry Vermouth and white wine and reduce the liquid by half. Now add the fish stock with the saffron and reduce this quantity by three-quarters. Pour in the cream, season and allow it to simmer for 2 minutes. Strain the saffron fish sauce through a fine sieve or muslin.

Score the tomatoes, plunge them into boiling water for 5–10 seconds, remove them and slip off the skins. Now de-seed them and roughly chop them up. Add the tomatoes to the sauce, put it back on the heat and simmer for around 3 minutes.

Meanwhile, steam all the fish and shellfish together for 3–4 minutes.

Pour some of the warm sauce on to each of the 4 serving plates. Place the rendezvous of fish and shellfish on top of the sauce and garnish with the herbs.

A glass of chilled Noilly Prat, enhanced with a little angostura bitters and lime, would make the ideal aperitif!

Hot and Sour Fish Stew

6 large shitake mushrooms, sliced
1 large carrot, peeled and cut into matchsticks
2 litres light chicken stock
thumb-sized piece of fresh root ginger, peeled
12 grinds of black pepper
2 tsp sesame oil
1 tbsp vinegar
1 tbsp dry sherry
1 tbsp soy sauce

1 small red chilli, chopped
100g frozen Birdseye peas
125g Heinz tomato ketchup
a selection of seafood (for example, tiger
  prawns, monkfish and scallops) weighing
  about 750g and cut up into bite-sized pieces
a small bunch of fresh coriander, chopped
1 egg, beaten
2 spring onions, chopped

Put the shitake mushrooms and carrots into a pan with the chicken stock, bring to the boil and simmer for 5 minutes.
Meanwhile, put the ginger, black pepper, sesame oil, vinegar, dry sherry, soy sauce and chilli in a liquidiser and blend.
When the mushrooms and carrots have been cooking for 10 minutes, add the peas and continue simmering for 3
more minutes. Now pour in the mixture from liquidiser, add the tomato ketchup and simmer for a further 5 minutes.
Next add the seafood pieces and simmer gently until the fish is lightly cooked.
Gently stir in the coriander and beaten egg and serve in warmed bowls with chopped spring onions on top.

Fillets of Salmon
served with a lentil, saffron, bean and potato broth

100ml fish stock
50g Puy lentils, cooked
50g haricot beans, cooked
100g fine green beans, trimmed and blanched
100g small new potatoes, cooked
1/2 tsp saffron
salt and pepper

4 x 185g salmon fillets, boned and with the skin
  on but scaled
10ml olive oil
40g plum tomatoes, diced
5g fresh chervil, chopped
5g fresh dill, chopped

Make the broth by bringing the fish stock to the boil, adding the lentils, haricot beans, green beans and new potatoes and simmering for 6 minutes. Add the saffron and season to taste.

Sear the salmon in hot olive oil, skin side down, for 4 minutes. Now turn the fish over and continue cooking for a further 2 minutes.

Just before serving, add the tomatoes, chervil and dill to the broth and then ladle it into 4 large serving bowls.

Place the salmon fillets on the broth and serve immediately.

Ginger and Coriander Baked Salmon

2 cloves of garlic
40g piece of fresh ginger
6 green chillies
$1/2$ tbsp mustard seeds
$1/2$ tbsp cumin seeds
3 tbsp sunflower or olive oil
$1/4$ tbsp red chilli powder

$1/2$ tbsp salt
$1/2$ tbsp cracked black pepper
25g fresh coriander, chopped
4 x 175g pieces of salmon

In a small food processor, grind the garlic, ginger and chillies into a paste. In a small frying pan, heat the mustard seeds and cumin seeds until mustard seeds start to pop.

Put the oil, red chilli powder, salt and black pepper in a bowl and mix thoroughly. Add the garlic, ginger and chilli paste and the mustard and cumin seeds, mix everything together and then add the coriander.

Put the fish in an ovenproof dish, pour the marinade over it and leave it to marinate in the fridge for 1 hour.

Preheat the oven to 200°C.

Without draining off the marinade, put the salmon in the oven and bake for 20 minutes.

Roast Lamb Rump
on a bed of roast aubergine and peppers

4 x 175g lamb rumps, fully trimmed

4 cloves of garlic, peeled and sliced

12 slices of smoked pancetta

1 large aubergine, chopped

4 red peppers, peeled, de-seeded and
  chopped

rind of ½ orange

150ml olive oil

20 small unpeeled new potatoes

50g unsalted butter

150ml crème fraîche

50g fresh basil

6 soft sun-dried tomatoes, including the oil

Begin 1 hour before cooking by making small cuts in the lamb and putting slices from two of the cloves of garlic in them. Wrap the meat in the pancetta and leave it to stand for an hour.

Preheat the oven to 250°C.

Put the chopped aubergine and peppers, the rest of the sliced garlic and the orange rind into a foil parcel and roast them in the oven for 1 hour until soft. Pour off the juices from the aubergine mixture and reserve them. Put the aubergine mixture aside to keep warm.

Boil the potatoes in salted water until tender. Drain the potatoes and toss them in the butter.

Roast the lamb for 14 minutes until pink and then allow it to rest for 10 minutes before slicing it.

Put some of the warm aubergine and pepper mixture on each of the 4 serving plates and top with the sliced lamb.

Blend the crème fraîche, basil, sun-dried tomatoes and aubergine juices together. Pour this over the lamb and serve with the new potatoes.

Quesadilla de Pollo (Tinga)

4 boned and skinless chicken breasts
1$\frac{1}{2}$ tsp fresh oregano
6 fresh bay leaves
1 fresh green chilli, de-seeded and chopped
1 onion, peeled and chopped
2 cloves of garlic, peeled and crushed
$\frac{1}{2}$ tin of smoked chipotle chilli (if this is not
   available, halve and de-seed two small green
   chillies, put them under a hot grill until the
   skins blacken slightly and then chop them up)

15ml vegetable oil
5 fresh tomatoes, skinned, de-seeded and
   chopped
1 green pepper, de-seeded and sliced
salt and pepper
4 x 25cm flour tortillas

Put the chicken breasts in enough water to cover them, add the oregano and bay leaves and boil over a fairly high heat for about 40 minutes. Remove the breasts from the pan and allow them to cool.

Make the salsa by frying the chilli, onion, garlic and chipolte chilli in half of the vegetable oil over a moderate heat for 2 minutes until the onions are soft and then add the tomatoes.

To make the 'Tinga', shred the cooked chicken, add it to the salsa and simmer for 15 minutes. Add the sliced green pepper and cook for a further minute or so until the pepper softens slightly.

Now shallow-fry the tortillas in the remaining vegetable oil for 2 minutes until slightly crisp.

Heat the grill to its highest temperature. Divide the Tinga between the 4 tortillas and flash each one under the grill for about 40 seconds each.

You could serve this on a bed of rice, topped with guacamole, sour cream and salsa.

Zuppa di Pesce

4 plum tomatoes
4 tbsp extra-virgin olive oil
50g fresh flat leaf parsley, finely chopped
2 cloves of garlic, finely chopped
1 or 2 fresh red chilli peppers, cut lengthwise
 and de-seeded
1 small onion, finely chopped
2 sticks celery, finely chopped
175ml dry white wine

1.5kg of fresh sea fish and shellfish cleaned,
 boned and cut into bite-sized pieces (This can
 be a mixture of monkfish, Dublin Bay prawns,
 a small lobster, calamari, cod, mussels,
 cockles, clams – anything that is available and
 that you like personally.)
2 fresh bay leaves
salt and pepper
4 servings of garlic bread

Score the skins of the tomatoes and put them into boiling water for 40 seconds, remove and plunge into cold water.
These can now be easily peeled, de-seeded and chopped.

In a large frying pan that will hold all of the ingredients, add the olive oil, heat it to a moderate temperature and then add
the parsley, garlic and the chilli pepper. Fry for about 1 minute and then add the onion, celery and tomatoes, taking
care not to burn them!

When this is well cooked and the tomatoes begin to break up, add the white wine and allow it to reduce for 2 minutes.

Add all of the fish and the bay leaves, season and add enough water to just cover everything.

Bring to the boil and cook until the mussels have all opened. If you are not using mussels, cook for 5 minutes.

Adjust the seasoning and serve with the garlic bread.

Roast Fillet of Buccleuch Beef
with sautéed wild mushrooms, truffled green beans and a balsamic vinegar jus

salt and pepper

4 x 175g portions of Buccleuch beef fillet (ask your butcher to get this for you)

100ml vegetable or olive oil

400g unsalted butter

600g Rosval potatoes, peeled (use Jersey Royals if the Rosval variety is not available

20g thyme

100ml water

50ml balsamic vinegar

50ml ready-made veal jus or beef stock

50ml truffle oil

400g shallots, chopped

200g mixed wild mushrooms

200g green beans, trimmed

50g fresh chervil

Preheat the oven to 200°C.

Season the beef. Heat the oil in a frying pan until it is smoking and seal the meat by allowing it to colour on each side. At the same time, over a moderate heat, melt 50g of the butter in another pan, add the potatoes and colour them.

Once the potatoes are golden, put them into an ovenproof dish and add some thyme, salt and pepper, 200g of butter and 100ml of water. Now put the potatoes in the oven and cook them for 20–25 minutes.

Transfer the beef fillets to a roasting tin. This is going in the oven at the same time as the potatoes but when you put it in the oven will depend on how well done you want it to be. It will take 15–20 minutes for medium, longer for well done and a shorter time for rare.

While the potatoes and beef are cooking, put a pot on the stove, add the balsamic vinegar and leave it to reduce by three-quarters. Once this is done, add the veal jus or beef stock and bring it to the boil.

Halfway through the cooking time, turn the beef so that it cooks evenly. You should also check the potatoes at this stage to make sure they are not overcooked. Take the potatoes out when they are tender and golden in colour. When the beef is cooked, take it out and leave it to rest.

Warm the truffle oil in a pan, add the shallots and cook until they are tender. Now add the wild mushrooms and continue cooking for 2–3 minutes on medium heat. Meanwhile, put green beans into boiling water and cook them for 3–4 minutes. Drain the beans and immediately add them to the pan with the shallots and mushrooms.

Put the beef under the grill to warm through. Place some of the shallot, mushroom and green bean mixture in the centre of 4 serving plates and then put three potatoes on each plate. Once the beef fillets are hot enough, remove them from the grill and put one on top of the vegetables. Finish the dish with balsamic sauce and garnish with the sprigs of chervil.

Enjoy.

Classic dishes with contemporary flavours are served in the stylish surroundings and ambience of Rococo.

Philosophy: to create an educated eating culture, featuring modern Scottish cooking with a subtle international influence and rustic Italian warmth.

rococo

Head chef Andrew Cumming is proud of Rogano's 'reputation as a Glasgow institution renowned worldwide for excellence'. The oldest surviving restaurant in Glasgow, it has a unique 1930s ambience. Luxurious fish and seafood dishes are elegantly presented in the Restaurant and Oyster Bar. The relaxing Café Rogano, with lighter dishes, is great for lunch or a pre-theatre meal with friends.

Philosophy: dedicated to the fine art of cooking and serving fish and seafood from Scottish waters.

rogano

Sea Bass with Scallop Mousse
served with chive beurre blanc

500g scallops
1 egg white
250ml double cream
sea salt
ground white pepper
4 sea bass fillets, scaled and boned
500ml fish stock

250ml dry white wine
10ml white wine vinegar
2 shallots, finely chopped
150g unsalted butter, cut up into 1cm cubes
1 bunch of fresh chives, finely chopped

Reserving 4 of the scallops as a garnish, blend the remaining scallops with the egg white in a blender or food processor. Then gradually add the double cream until a firm mousse has formed and finally add the seasoning. Preheat the oven to 200°C.

Roll the sea bass fillets into cylinder shapes and spoon the mousse mixture inside them. Place one of the reserved scallops on top of each cylinder and secure them with cocktail sticks. Place the fish in an ovenproof tray with half of the fish stock and cook in the oven for about 12–15 minutes.

Make the beurre blanc by putting the remaining fish stock, the white wine, the white wine vinegar and the chopped shallots in a pan and reduce the liquid to approximately 100ml. Sieve the reduced liquid and return it to a hot pan. Gradually add the cubes of butter to the reduced fish stock. Remove from the heat and whisk until a creamy sauce has formed. Finally, add the chopped chives and serve with the sea bass.

Roast Halibut and Buttered Leeks
with mussel and oyster fricassee

180g (4 portions) halibut

20 mussels, steamed and removed from shells

12 oysters, removed from shells, with juices
  collected

sprig of thyme

2 leeks, cut in circles

salt

pepper

300ml white wine

250g unsalted butter, plus a little more for
  cooking

2 shallots, sliced

1 lemon

extra-virgin olive oil

50g fresh chives and chervil, chopped

Place the sliced shallots and wine in a saucepan and reduce by half.

Add the thyme and whisk 250g of the butter in gradually. Add a squeeze of lemon juice, season with salt and pass through a sieve. Keep warm.

Heat a non-stick pan with enough extra-virgin olive oil to create a light film on the surface. Sear the halibut, rounded side down first. When golden brown, turn over, add a knob of butter and continue cooking until just done.

Sweat the leeks in the rest of the butter, seasoning well with salt and pepper. Cook until soft, without colouring.

Place a portion of the leeks in the centres of 4 serving dishes and gently place a portion of the halibut on top. Repeat with the remainder of the leeks and halibut.

Add the oysters, mussels and juice to the warm butter sauce, then the chopped chives and chervil. Heat thoroughly until the oysters and mussels are warmed through and pour the fricassee around the base of the dishes to finish.

Salt and Pepper Baby Squid
with a spiced tomato and mint salad on a humous plate

enough vegetable oil for deep-frying
200g fresh baby squid (rings and tails)
250g plain flour (seasoned with salt and pepper
  to taste)
1 small tub humous
2 unripened tomatoes, cut into large dice
2 large handfuls of rocket leaves
$^1/_2$ bunch fresh mint leaves, picked from stalks

$^1/_2$ bunch fresh coriander leaves, picked from
  stalks
3 tbsp tinned chickpeas
2 tbsp harissa
1 tbsp balsamic vinegar
1 tbsp extra-virgin olive oil
a little paprika

Heat the oil in a frying pan, chip pan or deep-fat fryer to a medium–hot heat (around 170°C–190°C) but make sure the oil is not smoking. Squeeze and toss the squid in the seasoned flour and then deep-fry it until a light golden brown. Spread the hummus over the bases of 4 serving plates.

Put all the other ingredients, except the paprika, in a bowl with the hot deep-fried squid, toss everything together and then pile it on top of the humous.

Sprinkle with paprika and serve.

Gaeng Khiaw Waan Goong
(Thai green curry with prawns)

675g fresh prawns, shelled and de-veined
2 shallots, chopped
4 cloves of garlic, chopped
25mm piece of fresh ginger, chopped
3 coriander roots, chopped
8 fresh red chillies, chopped
4 fresh small green chillies, chopped
2 stalks lemon grass, chopped
2 tbsp kaffir lime peel, chopped
10 black peppercorns

1 tsp coriander seeds
2 tsp cumin seeds
1 tsp shrimp paste
125ml coconut cream
350ml thick coconut milk
4 fresh basil leaves
4 kaffir lime leaves
2 tbsp fish sauce
2 tsp palm sugar
a handful of fresh coriander leaves

Wash the prawns, pat them dry and then set them aside.

Put the chopped shallots, garlic, ginger, coriander roots, chillies and lemon grass in a mortar and pound them gently. Now add the lime peel, peppercorns, coriander seeds, cumin seeds and shrimp paste and keep pounding till the mixture is smooth.

Boil the coconut cream, stirring continuously until the oil rises to the surface. Add the spice paste and stir over a moderately hot heat until the mixture is thick and fragrant.

Add the prawns and a third of the coconut milk and bring back to the boil. Stir in all the remaining coconut milk and then add the basil and lime leaves. Keep cooking until the liquid has reduced by a third and then add the fish sauce and sugar.

Transfer the curry to a serving bowl and garnish with the fresh coriander leaves.

thai fountain

Thai cooking is strongly influenced by the Chinese and its presentation, texture and taste vary from region to region. At the Thai Fountain this exquisite culinary art is taken to a new level. Delicate herbs, fragrant spices and lemongrass are blended together for a mouthwatering, subtle combination of Indian and Chinese cooking.
Philosophy: simplicity is the key!

quigley's

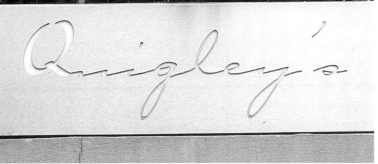

The creative environment of the kitchen at Quigley's has inspired John Quigley to produce original dishes such as the Coconut Rice Pudding he has contributed to *Gourmet Glasgow*. He believes in 'a healthier, more leisurely way of eating and more restaurants serving simple, natural food'.

This lively restaurant, in a city-centre town house, offers stylish food and a sophisticated atmosphere.

Quigley's Fishcakes
with tomato and basil salsa and rocket

200g potatoes, peeled and diced
300g salmon
300g haddock
60g breadcrumbs
1 medium egg, beaten
2 tbsp fresh parsley, chopped
2 tbsp fresh chives, chopped
salt
white pepper
flour, to dust

a little vegetable oil, for frying
16 cherry tomatoes, quartered
1 tbsp fresh basil, shredded
1 small red onion, finely diced
4 tbsp tomato ketchup
1 tbsp white wine vinegar
2 tbsp olive oil
salt and pepper
4 handfuls of rocket

Boil the potatoes in salted water, drain and cool.
Dice the raw salmon and raw haddock or coarsely chop them using the pulse setting of a blender or food processor.
Combine the fish, potatoes, breadcrumbs, egg, parsley, chives and salt and pepper to taste in large bowl and thoroughly mix. Mould the mixture into gateaux rings or, with clean hands, pat them into thick cakes. You should get 8 fishcakes from this quantity. Lightly dust the cakes with flour and then fry them over a medium heat in a lightly oiled non-stick pan for 8–10 minutes, turning them occasionally, until they are golden brown.
Combine the cherry tomatoes, basil, onion, ketchup, wine vinegar, olive oil, salt and pepper and mix well.
Divide the rocket between 4 plates, top with 2 fishcakes per plate and spoon on a generous dollop of salsa.

Port Zabaglione Ice Cream

4 egg yolks
150ml ruby port
225g castor sugar
250ml double cream

2 ripe Ogen melons
$\frac{1}{2}$ Honeydew melon
$\frac{1}{2}$ watermelon

Whisk the egg yolks with an electric whisk until they form thick ribbons.

Bring the port and 125g of the castor sugar to the boil and cook for 1 minute until it is syrupy. Pour the hot syrup on to yolks and keep whisking gently until the mixture is cold.

Whip the cream and fold it into the sabayon (the egg yolk and syrup mixture).

Wrap 4 individual stainless steel ring moulds in cling film and fill them with the sabayon cream and freeze.

Using a hand blender, purée one of the Ogen melons with the remaining 100g of sugar. Spread the melon coulis on 4 plates, de-mould the sabayon creams and place them on top.

Use a melon baller to form the rest of the melons into pearls and garnish the plates with them.

city café

This exciting contemporary restaurant, in a stunning waterfront location, concentrates on flavour and presentation. In summer, enjoy alfresco dining; in winter, there are fantastic river views from inside.

Philosophy: modern food, in relaxed surroundings.

Inspired by the abundance of Scotland's fresh seafood, the City Merchant's design and service is simple and casual. Head chef Tracy Bogle believes Glasgow's 'good name and reputation are well-deserved'.

Philosphy: bright, fresh, light design, quality ingredients, and food and service to match.

city merchant

Warm Pancakes
with ginger wine and brandy sauce and mascarpone ice cream

130g plain flour
pinch of salt
2 medium eggs
200ml milk mixed with 75ml water
195g unsalted butter
180g soft dark brown sugar

4 tbsp ginger wine
2 tbsp brandy
2 pieces of stem ginger, chopped
mascarpone ice cream
4 strawberries, halved but still joined at the
 leaves

To make the pancakes, sift the flour and salt into a large bowl. Make a well in the middle, break the eggs into it and mix together using a whisk or a fork. Gradually add the milk and water mixture, whisking continually until the mixture is smooth and is of a similar consistency to double cream.

Melt 65g of the butter in a small pot and then ladle 2 tbsp of the melted butter into the batter and mix well.

The remainder of the butter will be used to lubricate the small frying pan or skillet between cooking the pancakes. Lightly smear the frying pan/skillet with a little butter and place it on a low heat until it is slightly smoking. Pour approximately 2 tbsp of the batter into a small ladle so that it can be poured into the pan in one go. Tip the pan around from side to side to form a round pancake. When the batter firms on top and small air holes appear, use a palette knife to flip the pancake over. It should be golden brown in colour. Continue doing this until all the batter has been used up. Store the pancakes on a warm plate, using greaseproof paper to separate them.

To make the sauce, gently melt the remaining 130g of butter in a small pot, add the sugar and cook until the sugar has dissolved. Add the ginger wine, brandy and the chopped stem ginger and stir gently. Remove the sauce from the heat and keep it warm.

Fold the pancakes into quarters – you should have enough for 3 per person – and place them on the 4 serving plates. Spoon the sauce over them, place a ball of ice cream in the centre and garnish each with a strawberry.

Rose Panna Cotta with Raspberries

1 leaf of gelatine
3 tbsp granulated sugar
6 tbsp water
1 punnet of raspberries
500ml double cream

30g castor sugar
7–8 drops rose essence
icing sugar, for dusting

Soak the gelatine in enough cold water to cover it.

Put the granulated sugar and water in a pan, bring to the boil and cook until syrupy. Add a few of the raspberries and simmer for a few minutes. Push the liquid and raspberries through a sieve into a jug.

Bring the cream and castor sugar to the boil, reduce the heat and simmer very gently for 5 minutes. Remove the cream from heat and add the rose essence. Squeeze the water out of the gelatine, add it to the pan and stir until it has dissolved. Now sit the pan in a basin of cold water, stirring occasionally until the mixture has cooled.

Pour the cooled mixture into 4 pudding moulds or cups and leave them in the fridge to set for about 6 hours.

Dip each mould or cup in warm water before turning them out on to 4 serving plates. Garnish with the remaining raspberries and the raspberry syrup and then dust each plate with icing sugar.

If its quality cuisine and fine wines were not enough, Dining Room's seductive chocolate-brown and cherry-red decor creates an intimate atmosphere. The food, imaginatively prepared, entices and satisfies the palate. The standards it sets help fulfil chef and partner Jim Kerr's desire to help 'promote Glasgow as a whole'.

dining room

lux

The menus at Lux feature the best Scottish produce, cooked to perfection by chef and owner Stephen Johnson. Lux's reputation and success are based on stylish cuisine at good prices.
Philosophy: 'Heed the "customer comment" and improvement will follow.'

Strawberry Shortbread
with lemon mascarpone

450g unsalted butter
113g castor sugar
340g plain flour
113g cornflour
500g fresh strawberries, stalks removed and
  sliced

56g castor sugar
500g mascarpone cheese
juice of 1 lemon

To make the shortbread, cream the butter and sugar together. Add the flour and cornflour but do not over-mix. Wrap the dough in cling film and leave it to rest in the fridge for around 2 hours.

Preheat the oven to 180°C.

Now roll the pastry out to about 1.25cm thick, cut it into heart shapes and place these on a lightly floured but ungreased baking tray. Cook in the preheated oven for about 20 minutes until they are a light brown colour. Remove them from the oven, sprinkle them with castor sugar and allow them to cool on the baking tray.

To make the strawberry sauce, put half the strawberries in a bowl, add the castor sugar and purée with hand blender.

To make the lemon mascarpone, soften the cheese with spoon, mix it with the lemon juice and put it in a piping bag.

When the shortbread is cool, pipe a layer of cheese on to one piece of it, top with some strawberry slices and repeat the procedure until you have 3 pieces of shortbread on top of each other.

Place one triple-decker shortbread on each of the 4 serving plates and surround them with a small pool of strawberry sauce.

Banana Tarte Tatin

100g unsalted butter
250g brown sugar
150ml double cream
4 firm bananas, peeled and sliced at an angle to
  give 3cm-thick pieces

200g ready-made puff pastry, rolled out and cut
  into 4 circles
vanilla ice cream and fresh berries, to garnish

Put the butter and brown sugar in a pan over a medium heat and cook until the mixture caramelises. Remove from heat and mix in the cream to form a soft caramel sauce.

Preheat the oven to 280°C.

Pour the caramel into 4 non-stick tartlet cases and top with the banana slices so that all the caramel is covered. Place a puff pastry circle on top and seal round the edges.

Bake in the oven for about 12 minutes. Allow the tartlets to stand for 1 minute and then turn them upside down and remove from tart case while still warm.

Serve with the ice cream and berries.

Panna Cotta
with poached peppered strawberries

600ml double cream
25g castor sugar
1 vanilla pod, split and with the seeds scraped
 out
1¼ sheets of gelatine, soaked in cold water
 and then drained

25ml water
250g strawberries, hulled and sliced
50g castor sugar
5g cracked black pepper
12 strawberries, hulled and quartered
4 sprigs of fresh mint

Put the cream and sugar in a pan and heat until almost boiling. Add the soaked gelatine, stir it in and then leave it to cool. Pour the mixture into small circular moulds and chill them in the fridge overnight.

Bring the water to the boil, add the castor sugar, pepper and sliced strawberries and poach gently over a low heat for 10–15 minutes. Remove the pan from the heat and leave it to cool naturally. Pour the mixture through a fine sieve.

Turn the panna cottas out of their moulds on to 4 chilled serving plates. Pour strawberry coulis over the panna cottas, arrange the strawberry quarters around the plates, garnish each with a sprig of mint and serve.

Coconut Rice Pudding
with tropical fruit kebab and sweet chilli and passion fruit glaze

250g pudding rice
1 tin coconut milk
350ml milk
50g castor sugar
50ml Malibu
zest of 1 lime
1 banana, peeled and cut into chunks
1 mango, peeled, de-stoned and cut into
 chunks

1 paw-paw, peeled, de-seeded and cut into
 chunks
2 kiwi fruits, peeled and cut into chunks
4 tbsp ready-made sweet chilli sauce (maeploy)
2 passion fruits
1 tbsp fresh mint, chopped
juice of 1 lime

Combine the rice, coconut milk, milk, sugar, Malibu and lime zest in a pot and cook until the rice is soft and thick.

Skewer the fruit, except the passion fruits, in a repeated sequence on 6-inch bamboo skewers.

Combine the sweet chilli sauce and passion fruit pulp in pan, large enough to take the fruit kebabs, over high heat. When the liquid is bubbling, add the kebabs and cook until they are lightly caramelised on all sides. While the kebabs are still in the pan, sprinkle the mint and lime juice over them.

Mound the pudding rice in the centres of 4 serving plates, place the kebabs on top and drizzle the sauce over the plates.

Savoiarda alla Panna

500ml semi-skimmed milk

grated zest of ½ a lemon

4 egg yolks

75g castor sugar

2 tsp vanilla essence

50g plain flour, sifted

15ml rum or brandy

25g salted butter

200g savoiardi

400g sponge cake, cut up into 1–1.5cm slices

75ml coffee sambuca

75ml Strega (orange-flavoured Italian liqueur)

45ml apricot jam

30ml water

fresh whipped cream, for garnish

chopped toasted almonds, for garnish

To make the crème patisserie, put the milk and lemon zest into a small saucepan. Gently heat the milk and the lemon zest, removing the pan from the heat as soon as small bubbles start forming.

Beat the egg yolks with a wire whisk, gradually adding the sugar and vanilla essence. Continue beating until all the sugar has been incorporated and the mixture is smooth and pale yellow in colour. Next beat in the flour and then stir in the milk, pouring it through a strainer to remove the lemon zest.

When all the milk has been added, pour the mixture into a heavy-based pan and bring it to the boil, stirring constantly with a whisk. Once it is beginning to boil, turn the heat down and simmer for 5–6 minutes. Remove the pan from the heat and stir in the rum or brandy. Now beat in the butter and then leave it aside to cool. Stir the pan from time to time to prevent a skin forming on the crème patisserie.

Brush one side of the biscuits and cake slices with the coffee sambuca and brush the other sides with the Strega. Heat the jam and water together in a small pan.

Spread a layer of crème patisserie over the bottom of a serving dish and then put a layer of biscuits and cake slices on top. Pour the jam mixture over the layer of biscuits and cake slices. Continue with these layers of crème patisserie, biscuits and cake slices and jam mixture until all the ingredients have been used up, ending with a layer of crème patisserie.

Cover the dish with cling film or tin foil and put it in the fridge for 2–3 hours.

Spread the chopped almonds on a baking sheet and bake in a preheated oven at 200ºC for 5–10 minutes.

Decorate the top of the savoiarda alla panna with the whipped cream, topped with the chopped toasted nuts.

la fiorentina

La Fiorentina offers the finest Italian cuisine in charming surroundings with a friendly atmosphere. Their extensive menu of classic European and contemporary Mediterranean dishes incorporates the magical flavours of Tuscan cooking.

st.1989

0141·339 1944

SERIOUS

Small and unpretentious, this is a real hidden gem, one of Glasgow's best-kept secrets. So à la carte even the dishes are hand-washed to order . . . Comfy, cosy and intimate, serving fish with flair and desserts to die for. There's no need to dress up for this friendly, relaxed, informal West End venue. As for the two fat ladies, they couldn't possibly comment!

two fat ladies

Two Fat's Trio of Crème Brûlée

500ml double cream
1 vanilla pod, split
4 egg yolks
100g castor sugar

a handful of fresh raspberries
50ml Cointreau
a little extra castor sugar for caramelising
a small selection of fresh fruits for garnish

You wil need 12 individual-size ramekins for this dish.

Put the cream in a pan, scrape the seeds from the vanilla pod into the cream and then add the pod. Bring to the boil and cook gently until the cream has thickened slightly.

Mix the egg yolks with the sugar and beat until they are light and fluffy. Gradually and slowly add the boiled vanilla cream to the egg and sugar mixture, ensuring they are thoroughly combined. When all the cream has been mixed into the egg and sugar mixture, return it to the pan and put it on a low heat. Cook for about 5–10 minutes, until the brûlée mixture thickens, but take care not to allow it to boil.

Put a layer of raspberries in the bottom of 1 set of 4 ramekins and cover them with the brûlée mixture. Fill a second set of 4 dishes with the plain brûlée mixture. Add the Cointreau to the remaining brûlée mixture and use this to fill the remaining 4 ramekins. Put all 12 ramekins in the fridge to set.

Just before you are ready to serve, caramelise the tops by covering the surface with castor sugar and either grilling them until golden or glazing them with a kitchen blowtorch. Garnish with the fresh fruit.

contributor details

Amber Regent
50 West Regent
Street
Glasgow G2 2RA
0141 331 1655

L'Ariosto
92–4 Mitchell Street
Glasgow G1 3NQ
0141 221 0971

Ashoka (Ashton Lane)
19 Ashton Lane
Glasgow G12 8SJ
0800 195 3195

Ashoka (West End)
1284 Argyle Street
Glasgow G3 8AB
0800 195 3195

La Bonne Auberge
161 West Nile Street
Glasgow G1 2RL
0141 352 8310

Bouzy Rouge Casual Gourmet Dining
111 West Regent
Street
Glasgow G2 2RU
0141 221 8804

Bouzy Rouge Seafood & Grill
De Quincy House
71 Renfield Street
Glasgow G2 6AE
0141 333 9725

Café Andaluz
2 Cresswell Lane
Glasgow G12 8AA
0141 339 1111

Café Gandolfi
64 Albion Street
Glasgow
G1 1NY
0141 552 6813

Café Máo
84 Brunswick Street
Glasgow G1 1ZZ
0141 564 5161

Camerons
Hilton Glasgow
1 William Street
Glasgow G3 8HT
0141 204 5555

City Café
Finnieston Quay
Glasgow G3 8HN
0141 227 1010

City Merchant
97–9 Candleriggs
Glasgow G1 1NP
0141 553 1577

Dining Room
41 Byres Rd
Glasgow G11 5RG
0141 339 3666

étain
The Glass House
Springfield Court
Glasgow G1 3JN
0141 225 5630

La Fiorentina
2 Paisley Road West
Glasgow G51 1LE
Tel: 0141 420 1585

Frango
The Italian Centre
15 John Street
Glasgow G1 1HP
0141 552 4433

Gamba
225a West George
Street
Glasgow G2 2ND
0141 572 0899

Lux
1051 Great Western
Road
Glasgow G12 OXP
0141 576 7576

The Mariner
Glasgow Moat House
Hotel
Congress Road
Glasgow G3 8QT
0141 306 9988

Mother India
28 Westminster
Terrace
Glasgow G3 7RU
0141 221 1663

Mussel Inn
157 Hope Street
Glasgow G2 2UQ
0141 572 1405

OKO
The Todd Building
68 Ingram Street
Glasgow G3 7UL
0141 572 1500

Opus
150 St Vincent Street
Glasgow G2 5NE
0141 204 1150

La Parmigiana
44–7 Great Western
Road
Glasgow G12 8HN
0141 334 0686

Pancho Villas
26 Bell Street
Glasgow G1 1LG
0141 552 7737

Papingo
104 Bath Street
Glasgow G2 2EN
0141 332 6678

Quigley's
158–66 Bath Street
Glasgow
G2 4TB
0141 331 4061

Rococo
202 West George
Street
Glasgow G2 2NR
0141 221 5004

Rogano
11 Exchange Place
Glasgow G1 3AN
0141 248 4055

Saint Jude's
190 Bath Street
Glasgow G2 4HG
0141 352 8800

78 St Vincent
78 St Vincent Street
Glasgow G2 5UB
0141 248 7878

Stravaigin
28 Gibson Street
Glasgow G2 8NX
0141 334 2665/7165

Thai Fountain
2 Woodside Crescent
Glasgow G3 7UL
0141 332 1599/2599

Two Fat Ladies
88 Dumbarton Road
Glasgow G11 6NX
0141 339 1944

index